NEWLY UPDATED
CALGARY

TRAVEL GUIDE 2023

Your ultimate guide for visiting Canada's Finest City from where to stay, when to visit, things to do, and what to pack as a visitor

BY

JOAN A. PEARL

TABLE OF CONTENT

INTRODUCTION

Why is Calgary a must-see destination?

Calgary, Alberta, Canada, is a must-see location for anyone seeking to discover the great outdoors, experience Western Canadian culture, and luxuriate in a varied variety of gastronomic pleasures. Calgary is Alberta's biggest metropolis and is known as the entryway to the Canadian Rockies, making it an ideal beginning place for any adventurer. In this piece, we will look at why Calgary is a must-see location and why you should include it in your trip plans.

The Outstanding Outdoor

Calgary is an outdoor enthusiast's dream, with an abundance of outdoor activities accessible all year. During the winter, you can hit the slopes at one of the neighboring Rocky Mountains' many world-class snow destinations. Banff, a famous winter location, is only an hour and a half journey from Calgary. Snowshoeing, ice dancing, and even a horse-drawn carriage trip through a wintry paradise are all options.

Calgary is the ideal summer destination for exploring the great outdoors. Hiking through the gorgeous Canadian Rockies, biking along the Bow River, or exploring the area's numerous regional parks are all options. White-water kayaking down the Bow River is one of the most popular sports, providing an exciting experience for adventure enthusiasts.

Culture of Western Canada

Calgary is also renowned for its Western Canadian culture, which is reflected in the city's buildings, institutions, and yearly events. The Heritage Park Historical Village is a must-see site that allows visitors to live life in the late 1800s and early 1900s. The Glenbow Museum, which includes displays of Western Canadian history, art, and culture, is also worth a visit. The Calgary Stampede is a yearly celebration of Western Canadian culture and one of the world's biggest rodeos. The Stampede is held every July and includes rodeos, music, and a procession. It is a must-see gathering for anyone interested in Western Canadian culture.

Delights in the Kitchen

Calgary is also a foodie's utopia, with a wide variety of gastronomic treats to choose from. The city has a flourishing eatery culture, offering everything from traditional Canadian fare to foreign fare. Charbar, situated in the iconic Simmons Building and serving Argentinean-inspired food, is one of the must-visit eateries. The River Café, situated in Prince's Island Park, is another famous eatery that serves fresh Canadian food. If you want to try something new, go to the Calgary Farmers' Market, which has over 80 exhibitors offering fresh fruit, livestock, and specialty foods. The market is open all year and is a wonderful location to try out some native Canadian food.

To summarize, Calgary is a must-see location for anyone interested in exploring the great outdoors, experiencing

Western Canadian culture, and indulging in a wide variety of gastronomic pleasures. Whether you're looking for excitement, culture, or cuisine, the metropolis has something for everyone. Calgary should be on your trip plan because of its closeness to the Canadian Rockies and lively city culture.

Useful Information For Visitors

Planning a trip to a new place can be exciting and overwhelming at the same time. To make sure your experience is as pleasant as possible, it's important to familiarize yourself with the location's climate, time zone, currency, and any other notable information. Here's a guide to some useful information for visitors.

CLIMATE

Calgary, Alberta, Canada's temperature is categorized as an arid continental climate. Summers are hot and bright, with temps varying from 20 to 25 degrees Celsius (68 to 77 degrees Fahrenheit). Winters are chilly and arid, with average temps of -10°C (14°F). Calgary has 326 days of sunlight on average per year, making it one of the sunniest towns in Canada. In addition, the city gets an average of 599 millimeters (23.6 in) of precipitation per year, with the bulk of it falling during the summer months. Winter snowfall is frequent, with an average of 92 centimeters (36 in) per season. In the winter, Calgary gets precipitation and times of severe weather.

As a visitor to Calgary, I had a nice encounter with the weather. Summers in the city are very pleasant, with balmy, sunlit days, and winters are chilly but dry. I was able to enjoy the sunlight and tour the city without being concerned about excessive temperatures or pollution. I also got to witness ice and cyclones, which added to the excitement of my stay. Overall, the weather in Calgary was ideal for exploring and enjoying all that the city has to offer.

TIME ZONE

Calgary is in the United States and Canada's Mountain Time Zone. This implies that Calgary's schedule is two hours behind the Coordinated Universal schedule.

(UTC). This also means that Calgary observes daylight saving time, with the clock rising one hour in the spring and going back one hour in the autumn. Make careful to change your timepiece depending on when you intend to travel to Calgary.

For example, at noon UTC, Calgary's time is 10:00 am. When daylight saving time is followed in the spring, the time in Calgary is 11:00 am at noon UTC. In the autumn, Calgary's time is 9:00 a.m. to 12:00 pm UTC.

CURRENCY

Calgary, Canada's money is the Canadian dollar. (CAD). The Canadian dollar, which is split into 100 bits, is the legal money of Canada and its regions and territories. At the moment, one Canadian dollar is worth 0.73 US dollars. (USD).

The currency of Calgary is accepted throughout the city, and it's easy to find ATMs and banks to exchange currency. Money conversion services are also available in the area. It's important to note that some businesses may only accept cash, while others may accept both cash and credit cards.

When going to Calgary, make sure you have enough Canadian currency on hand. Additionally, you may want to exchange some of your home currency for Canadian dollars before you arrive. You'll have some native money for your journey this way.

EMERGENCY CONTACTS

In the case of an emergency in Calgary, having access to vital contact numbers for fast help is critical. Here is a list of Calgary emergency contacts:

1. **Emergency Services** (Police, Fire, and Ambulance): 911.

2. **Non-Emergency Police Assistance:** 403-266-1234 Calgary Police Service

3. **Medical Emergencies:** Call 811 (for non-emergency medical advice and information).

AHS's 24-hour Health Link number is 811 (for non-life-threatening crises).

4. **Poison Control:** 1-800-332-1414 (Alberta Poison and Drug Information Service).

5. **Calgary Distress Centre** (24-Hour Crisis Support): 403-266-HELP (4357)
1-877-303-2642 (Mental Health Helpline)

6. **Calgary Emergency Management Agency:** 311 (inside Calgary) or 403-268-2489 (outside Calgary) General Inquiries: 403-268-5521 Emergency Management: 403-268-5521

7. **Emergency Management:** 310-0000 Alberta Emergency Management Agency (In Alberta, toll-free). It's essential to remember that these emergency contacts are subject to change, so staying up to speed with the most recent contact information is always a smart idea. Furthermore, if you are at a particular place or institution, be

aware of any on-site emergency contacts or processes.

Remember to phone 911 if you are in a life-threatening emergency. Contact the proper agencies in non-emergency circumstances to guarantee prompt and appropriate help.

Travel Requirements

Calgary is a lively metropolis in the Canadian state of Alberta. It is well-known for its beautiful scenery, outdoor activities, and lively culture. There are a few journey criteria that must be fulfilled previous to entry for those planning to explore Calgary.

To begin, all tourists must have a current passport and permit. Visas are needed for all foreign tourists, and based on their place of birth, some visitors may also require an Electronic Travel Authorization (eTA). Visas must be acquired ahead of time, so it is critical to prepare ahead and file for the required papers as soon as feasible.

Visitors may also be required to show evidence of adequate funds for the length of their stay. A bank account, credit card, or other evidence of cash capacity is acceptable. Before landing in Calgary, make sure you have a return ticket and proper travel insurance.

Finally, because of the present COVID-19 epidemic, tourists should be informed of any limitations or rules in place. This may include a required self-quarantine time upon entry, a null COVID-19 test result, or evidence of immunization.

Visitors can guarantee a seamless trip to and from Calgary by following these transport criteria. Furthermore, these standards are open to change, so it is critical to remain current on any new laws before going.

My experience with Calgary's trip needs has been good. I was able to acquire the required papers in preparation, such as my passport and visa. Furthermore, I was able to plan for COVID-19 pandemic laws such as the required self-quarantine time and evidence of null COVID-19 test findings. Overall, I am confident that I am following all of the required laws and can plan my journey to Calgary with confidence.

Travel Restrictions

There are no travel restrictions for properly vaccinated tourists entering Calgary, Alberta, Canada as of March 8, 2023. Unvaccinated tourists must provide documentation of a COVID-19 test that was negative within 72 hours of arrival. Before arriving, all passengers must complete the ArriveCAN app or website.

The following are Calgary's particular travel restrictions:

- No testing or quarantine is necessary for fully vaccinated passengers.

- Unvaccinated visitors must provide documentation of a negative COVID-19 test within 72 hours of arrival. Upon arrival, you must be quarantined for 14 days.

- Children under the age of 12: There is no need for testing or quarantine, regardless of vaccination status.

Here are some more things to consider before visiting Calgary:

- No masks are necessary in public spaces.
- Social isolation is not encouraged in public spaces.
- Because the COVID-19 situation in Calgary is continuously changing, it is critical to review the most recent travel restrictions before departing.

Here is some other tourist advice when visiting Calgary:

- Plan ahead of time for your flights and lodgings, particularly if you're visiting during the high season.
- Pack comfy shoes since you will be walking a lot.
- Bring sunscreen and a hat since Calgary can become hot in the summer.

- Be prepared for large crowds. Because Calgary is a famous tourist destination, it may get congested at times.
- Have a good time! Calgary is a fantastic place to visit since it has something for everyone.

Visa and Passports

If you intend to journey to Calgary, Alberta, Canada, you must have a current passport and visa. Citizens of nations other than Canada, the United States, and Mexico usually needed to obtain a visa. If you are a resident of one of these countries, you can enter Canada without a visa if you have a legitimate passport and evidence of your intention to depart Canada after your stay.

When filing for a visa to enter Canada, you must provide comprehensive information about your intended reason for travel, anticipated duration of time, and location. You will also be required to provide personal information, such as your complete name, date of birth, and visa details. Visitors may also be required to show evidence of financial security, undergo a physical examination, and obtain a letter of introduction from a Canadian citizen.

If you are visiting Calgary for business, you may be required to acquire a work visa. This visa enables you to operate in Canada for a limited duration. You must provide evidence of an employment contract from a Canadian business, proof of the job's wage, and proof of the employer's capacity to pay the income to receive a work visa.

Before traveling to Calgary, make sure you have all of the required papers. Check that you have a current passport, visa, and, if necessary, work authorization. This will greatly simplify the procedure of accessing Canada.

Language

When you land in Calgary, you will notice that the city is rich in different ethnicities and dialects. Although

English is the most commonly spoken language in Calgary, many other languages include French, German, Spanish, Tagalog, and Punjabi. If you intend to remain in Calgary for a prolonged length of time, learning some of the native dialects may be helpful.

Here are some easy words that you can use in Calgary:

Hello, and good day. (in English)

Goodbye: Farewell (in English)

Please: S'il vous plait (in French)

Thank you very much: Merci (in French)

Yes: Ya (in Punjabi)

No, Nahi. (in Punjabi)

Please excuse me: Con permiso (in Spanish)

Do you understand English? : Hablas inglés? (in Spanish)

These words will assist you in navigating the city and communicating with residents. Learning a few native languages can help you interact with the people of Calgary and make your stay more pleasant.

My interactions with the Calgary vernacular have been excellent. I've had the chance to acquire some fundamental words in French, German, Spanish, Tagalog, and Punjabi. Learning these languages has made it easier for me to converse and bond with the natives. It has also made me comprehend the city and its customs better. Overall, acquiring Calgary's language has been a fantastic experience.

These are the fundamental components of knowledge you should gather before traveling to a new location. To ensure a pleasant and stress-free journey, acquaint yourself with the area's temperature, time zone, money, permits, language, transit, and safety.

Sim Cards and Sim Roaming

It was my first time in Calgary, and I was eager to see what the city had to offer. I'd heard so many positive things about the metropolis and couldn't wait to see it for myself. But before I could do anything, I needed to get a Sim card and configure Sim roaming.

I had never done anything like this before, so I was a little apprehensive. I went to a shop and inquired for assistance. The shop employee was pleasant and gentle, and he described the complete procedure to me. He handed me a Sim card and showed me how to set it up for traveling. He also advised me on which network to use, as some networks are better suited to specific applications.

I felt relaxed and eager to explore the city after I finished setting up the Sim card and traveling. The stunning landscape and welcoming people wowed me. I was able to remain in touch with my family and coworkers wherever I traveled, and I found it easy to navigate.

I had a wonderful time in Calgary thanks to the Sim card and Sim traveling. It was a fantastic encounter, and I was grateful to have received the assistance I required.

A SIM device and SIM roaming are required for first-time visitors to Calgary. With a SIM card, you can use your smartphone to make conversations, exchange messages, and browse the internet while in the city. SIM roaming enables you to use your home phone number while traveling, allowing you to contact and receive messages from family and friends back home. Here's an explanation of SIM cards and SIM travel in Calgary.

What exactly is a SIM card?

A SIM card (Subscriber Identity Module) is a device that saves your phone number, contacts, and other information. It allows you to connect to the cell network and use your smartphone to make conversations, exchange messages, and browse the internet.

What exactly is SIM Roaming?

SIM roaming is a tool that enables you to use your home phone number while visiting another nation. This function comes in handy when you need to contact or receive messages from relatives and acquaintances back home.

Where Can I Get a SIM Card in Calgary?

To obtain a SIM card in Calgary, you must first ensure that your smartphone is enabled. Then you can get a SIM card at a neighborhood shop or online. Choose a package that is appropriate for your requirements and money.

How Do I Enable SIM Roaming in Calgary?

Once you have your SIM card, you can enable SIM roaming in Calgary by going to your phone's options and choosing "Roaming." Then, input the name of the nation you're visiting (for example, Canada) as well as your home phone number. Within a few minutes, your SIM roaming should be enabled.

Overall, first-time visitors to Calgary require a SIM card and SIM roaming. With a SIM card, you can use your smartphone to make conversations, exchange messages, and browse the internet. And, with SIM roaming, you can contact family and friends back home by using your home phone number while traveling.

where can I get a phone sim in Calgary?

A SIM card can be purchased in Calgary from any local cellphone carrier or online. Telus, Bell, Rogers, Koodo, and Fido are among the most popular service companies in Calgary. Pre-paid SIM cards are also available at convenience shops, supermarket stores, and other shopping locations.

And how much does a SIM card cost in Calgary?

The price of a SIM card in Calgary differs according to the supplier and package you select. In general, you can anticipate spending between $10 and $50 for a SIM card. Furthermore, some companies give pre-paid options starting at $15 per month.

In Calgary, I bought my SIM card from a Telus shop. I selected a plan that met my requirements and money, and the shop personnel was extremely helpful in describing the various choices. I also inquired about any extra costs or rebates that might be offered. I was able to enable SIM roaming in Calgary after purchasing my SIM card and package by choosing the "Roaming" option in my phone options.

Considering Using An Inverter And Converter

As a visitor to Calgary, you should be informed of the various kinds of converters and inverters accessible. Converters shift the power of a receptacle from one type to another, whereas inverters turn direct current (DC) to alternating current (AC). (AC). Knowing which sort to use is critical for ensuring that your gadgets function correctly.

Converters are used to convert the power of one sort of receptacle to another. A step-down converter, which lowers the power of a receptacle from 220V to 110V, is the most prevalent form of converter used in Calgary. This is required for products that require 110V, such as notebook computers and phones.

Inverters transform direct current (DC) to alternating current (AC). (AC). This is required for products that require AC to work correctly, such as cameras and other gadgets. Inverters come in several forms and sizes and can be used in automobiles, watercraft, and recreational vehicles.

Where Can I Purchase Converters and Inverters in Calgary?

In Calgary, most electrical shops sell converters and transformers. You can also buy them online from a variety of stores. It is critical to buy the proper variety for your gadget and thoroughly study the directions before using it.

In Calgary, I had a good encounter with converters and inverters. I required both kinds of devices for my laptop, phone, and camera and was able to quickly buy them from a nearby shop. The employees there were extremely helpful in describing the various kinds offered and ensuring that I had the correct ones for my devices.

Overall, it was a fantastic experience, and I was able to use my gadgets with no problems.

The price of a converter and transformer in Calgary differs according to style and size. In general, a converter will cost between $10 and $50, and an inverter will cost between $30 and $200.

Furthermore, some merchants provide rebates or package offers when buying both a converter and an inverter.

In Calgary, I bought my converter and transformer from a neighborhood electrical shop. I went with a package offer that included both a converter and a transformer for a total of $50. The shop employees were extremely helpful in describing the various kinds of converters and inverters available and ensuring that I had the correct ones for my devices.

CHAPTER 1: GETTING TO KNOW CALGARY

Calgary is a thriving metropolis in Alberta, Canada. It has a varied community of more than 1.3 million people and is well-known for its world-class sights, amusement, and outdoor activities. Calgary is a wonderful location for people of all ages, thanks to its flourishing economy, varied culture, and wealth of recreational activities. Calgary has something for everyone, from the magnificent Rocky Mountains to the varied neighborhoods and busy central center. Calgary is the ideal location to visit if you're looking for an excursion, a peaceful vacation, or thrilling entertainment.

A brief history of Calgary

Calgary is a thriving and varied metropolis with a long and illustrious past. This community, located in Alberta, was once a significant location for the Blackfoot and Cree peoples. European residents came in the late nineteenth century, and the metropolis expanded gradually over time. Calgary is now a contemporary and busy metropolis with more than 1.2 million residents.

Calgary's past can be traced back to the early nineteenth century when fur merchants and adventurers arrived in the region. The community was established as a municipality in 1884 after the first regular residents came in 1875. When the Canadian Pacific Railway established a stop in Calgary in the late 1800s, the city witnessed economic growth. This signaled the start of the city's transition from a sleepy village to a busy metropolis.

Calgary witnessed a surge of emigrants, mainly from Eastern Europe and Asia, in the early 1900s. This surge of immigrants influenced the city's culture, and Calgary is now a cosmopolitan metropolis with over 200 languages spoken within its boundaries.

In the mid-twentieth century, the metropolis experienced significant growth. The Calgary structure, a 626-foot viewing structure that is now one of the city's most recognized features, was built in the 1950s. The University of Calgary was founded in the 1960s, and the community proceeded to expand and flourish.

Calgary is a flourishing metropolis with varied industries today. It has evolved into a center for the energy, banking, and technology sectors, as well as a lively artistic environment. Calgary is an exciting and lively city that is bound to captivate the affection of its tourists with its rich heritage, varied culture, and a busy economy.

The population of Calgary

Calgary is the fifth-largest metropolis in Canada with a population of 1,237,656 as of 2020. Calgary is a lively and developing metropolis in the state of Alberta. It has a multicultural populace from all over the globe, including individuals from Canada, the United States, Europe, Asia, and Africa.

Calgary's populace has grown significantly over the years. Over the last decade, the population has increased by more than 10%. This development is primarily due to an inflow of individuals from other areas of Canada and the United States. Furthermore, Calgary has become a famous location for emigrants, with people arriving from all over the globe in quest of new possibilities.

Calgary is also attracting an increasing number of young workers, families, and seniors. Calgary attracts people who want to establish a company, raise a family, or retire in a secure and lively metropolis. The city's economy is varied and thriving, with employment in the oil and gas sector, technology, banking, and healthcare.

Calgary is an excellent city in which to reside and establish a family. It has a robust economy, low jobless rates, an excellent education system, and a wide range of cultural, leisure, and amusement opportunities. Furthermore, Calgary is a lovely metropolis with many parks and natural areas, a lively central area, and a variety of activities to keep everyone amused.

To summarize, Calgary is an excellent location to reside. It has a diverse community of individuals from all over the globe, a robust industry, and a wide range of activities for everyone. If you're searching for a new location to live, Calgary might be the place for you.

The Culture and Traditions of Calgary

Calgary is a lively city with a rich past and culture. From concerts and events to museums and art galleries, there is something for everyone to enjoy. The city is full of unique customs that have been handed down through centuries, and each one is a testimony to the city's varied culture.

One of the city's most famous events is the Calgary Stampede, which is held each year in July. The event is a festival of Western culture and history, with rodeos, live music, and engaging activities. It's one of the biggest events in the nation and a great chance to sample Western culture.

The Calgary International Film Festival is another famous event that honors the city's art and culture. The festival features some of the best films from around the globe and is an excellent chance to experience the unique culture of the city.

The Calgary Tower is one of the city's most famous symbols. The viewing deck offers a stunning 360-degree view of the city and its neighboring scenery. The tower also acts as an emblem of the city's past and culture, with its vivid lights and vibrant design.

Calgary is also home to a range of museums and art venues. These places provide a chance to examine the city's past and culture in greater depth. The Glenbow Museum, for example, is home to over one million relics and offers a range of displays and events.

These are just a few of the many ethnic and customary pursuits offered in Calgary. From concerts and events to museums and art galleries, there is something for everyone to experience. Calgary is a lively city with a rich past and culture and is a great spot to travel and find.

My experience with the culture and customs of Calgary has been extremely good. I have had the chance to explore the city's rich past and culture through concerts, events, museums, and art galleries. I have also learned more about the city's famous sites, such as the Calgary Tower. I have greatly loved my stay here and have gotten a better respect for the city's varied culture.

One example of the culture and customs in Calgary is the Calgary Stampede. This is a yearly event that honors Western culture and history with rodeos, live music, and engaging activities. Additionally, the Calgary International Film Festival is a great chance to experience the city's art and culture. The Calgary Tower is also an emblem of the city's past and culture, with its vivid lights and vibrant design. Finally, museums and art galleries provide a chance to examine the city's past and culture in greater depth.

Some of the artistic and customary events in Calgary occur throughout the year, such as museums and art exhibits. However, some events, such as the Calgary Stampede, take place at a precise time of year. Additionally, some concerts and events are only held yearly, so if you're interested in going it's essential to plan prior.

The Customs and Religion of Calgary

Calgary is a multicultural community with a long past. Because of its big population, the city is home to a diverse range of ethnicities and faiths. Learning about Calgary's traditions and faith can help tourists obtain a better understanding of this lively city.

When it comes to traditions, Calgary is a blend of conventional and contemporary. Traditional clothing, such as tartan, is still worn openly in some regions. Then there's the fact that if you're looking for a way to save money, this is the place to be.

Religion is very significant in Calgary. The metropolis is home to many faith groups, including Christians, Muslims, Jews, Hindus, and Buddhists. Each faith has its own set of ideas and customs, and many Calgary residents participate in religious events.

Aside from traditions and faith, Calgary is renowned for its thriving arts and music communities. Many Calgary residents attend the city's numerous events, including the Calgary Folk Music Festival and the Calgary International Film Festival. There are also numerous art studios and institutions in the metropolis.

Calgary is a lively metropolis with a varied range of traditions, faiths, and ethnicities. Understanding these traditions and faiths can help tourists obtain a better understanding of the city and its inhabitants.

My interactions with Calgary's traditions and faith have been excellent. I've had the chance to learn about the city's conventional and contemporary traditions, as well as its many faith groups. I've also had the opportunity to visit events and learn about the city's lively arts and music communities. Learning about Calgary's traditions and faith has helped me acquire a better understanding of this lively metropolis.

Here is a summary of some of Calgary's temples and mosques:

Churches:
- Church of the First Alliance
- The Cathedral of St. Mary
- The Anglican Church of St. Stephen
- Knox United Methodist Church
- Southwood United Methodist Church
- Baptist Church of West Hillhurst

Mosques:
- Calgary Islamic Centre Al Madinah Mosque of Baitun Nur
- Islamic Centre of Calgary
- Masjid Madinah
- Masjid Al-Huda
- Al-Salam Masjid

I had the chance to visit First Alliance Church while in Calgary. Learning about Christianity and connecting with the local community was a fantastic experience. The chapel was warm and inviting, as were the residents. I was also able to visit St. Mary's Cathedral, St. Stephen's Anglican Church, Knox United Church, Southwood United Church, and West Hillhurst Baptist Church.

If someone is considering a trip to Calgary, I would counsel them to do their homework on the city's temperature, time zone, money, permits, language, transit, and safety. Additionally, it's essential to acquaint yourself with the city's traditions and faiths, as well as its lively art and music scenes. Finally, make time to visit the city's many sites and get to know the residents.

CHAPTER 2: WHAT TO KNOW BEFORE TRAVELING

Best Time To Visit

As a first-time traveler to Calgary, it's essential to know the ideal time to explore. The city experiences a variety of conditions and temperatures throughout the year, so the scheduling of your journey will depend on the sort of activities you plan to do. Here's a guide to the ideal time to explore Calgary as a first-timer.

Spring (March-May) is a wonderful season to explore Calgary. The temperature is pleasant and the days are growing longer, making it the optimal season for outdoor activities. It's also a wonderful opportunity to discover the city's many parks and pathways.

Summer (June - August) is a perfect season to explore Calgary. The weather is mild and bright, making it the ideal season for outdoor activities such as trekking, bicycling, and paddling.

Additionally, this is the ideal time to experience the city's many celebrations and activities.

Fall (September - November) is another excellent season to explore Calgary. The temperature is colder and the days are growing shorter, making it the perfect season for experiencing the city's many cultural destinations, such as museums and galleries.
Additionally, this is the ideal time to take advantage of the city's many outdoor activities.

Winter (December - February) is also a fantastic season to explore Calgary. The weather can be chilly, but the days are shortened, making it the perfect season for experiencing the city's many interior destinations.
Additionally, this is the ideal time to take advantage of the city's many winter activities, such as snowboarding and snowmobiling.

Overall, the ideal time to explore Calgary as a first-timer will depend on the sort of activities you intend to do. Spring, summer, autumn, and winter all offer distinct experiences, so make sure you organize your journey appropriately.

I explored Calgary in the summer. The weather was mild and bright, making it the optimal season for outdoor activities such as trekking, bicycling, and paddling. Additionally, this was the ideal time to experience the city's many celebrations and events. I had a wonderful experience and would recommend visiting Calgary in the summer.

My advice for others visiting Calgary is to organize your journey according to the sort of activities you intend to do. Each season provides distinct experiences, so make sure you organize your journey appropriately. Additionally, make sure to verify the temperature before you go and carry the appropriate garments and materials. Finally, don't neglect to make duplicates of your identification and other essential paperwork before you depart home.

Where To Stay

As a first traveler visiting Calgary, you'll want to make sure that you locate the optimal location to remain while you experience this dynamic city. From the breathtaking Rocky Mountains to the bustling downtown region, there is so much to see and do in Calgary. With so many different accommodation choices to choose from, it can be challenging to determine where to remain in Calgary. Here is an introduction to the finest locations to remain in Calgary as a first visitor.

1. Downtown Calgary: Downtown Calgary is the optimal location to remain as a first traveler. Home to a vast assortment of stores, restaurants, and entertainment choices, this is the perfect location to discover. From the famous Calgary Tower to the bustling Stephen Avenue pedestrian plaza, there is something for everyone in the downtown region. Many of the downtown motels are also within strolling distance of Calgary's renowned destinations, making it an ideal location to remain.

2. Beltline District: Located just south of downtown, the Beltline District is a bustling and colorful neighborhood. Home to an assortment of fashionable restaurants, clubs, and retailers, this is the perfect location for a first visit to discover. With its tree-lined avenues and picturesque architecture, the Beltline District is also a wonderful location to remain in Calgary.

3. East Village: Located in the center of downtown, East Village is a bustling and up-and-coming neighborhood. Home to a variety of fashionable restaurants, retailers, and galleries, it's a fantastic location to remain in for a first traveler. It's also within strolling distance of the Calgary Tower, Stampede Park, and the Bow River.

4. Mount Royal: If you're searching for a more peaceful location to remain in Calgary, then Mount Royal may be a perfect choice. Located on the western fringe of the city, Mount Royal is a tranquil and attractive neighborhood. With its tree-lined avenues and breathtaking vistas of the Rocky Mountains, it's a wonderful location to remain in for a first visit.

No matter where you remain in Calgary, you'll be sure to have an incredible time experiencing this bustling metropolis. From the bustling downtown region to the tranquil Mount Royal neighborhood, Calgary has something for everyone. So take your time to discover the finest locations to remain in Calgary as a first visit and enjoy your stay!

Budget-Friendly Options:

1. HI Calgary City Capital - Located just steps away from the city capital, HI Calgary City Centre provides clean and comfortable accommodation without breaking the budget.

2. International Hotel and Suites Calgary - This hotel provides a wonderful assortment of facilities and is situated just minutes away from downtown.

3. Econo Lodge Downtown - With its accessible position and excellent value for money, Econo Lodge Downtown is an excellent budget-friendly choice for lodging in Calgary.

Luxury Options:

1. Fairmont Palliser - Located in the center of downtown, the Fairmont Palliser is a sophisticated and fashionable hotel providing top-notch facilities.

2. Hyatt Regency Calgary - Located on the outskirts of downtown, the Hyatt Regency Calgary is a five-star hotel providing sumptuous accommodations with breathtaking vistas of the city.

3. The Westin Calgary - This hotel is situated in the center of downtown and provides a sumptuous stay with its top-notch facilities and dedicated employees.

Types Of Accommodation Available In Calgary?

There are a variety of different kinds of accommodation accessible in Calgary, depending on your income and inclinations. Here are some of the most prevalent kinds of accommodation in Calgary:

1. Hotels - Hotels are the most popular form of accommodation in Calgary, providing comfortable and accessible locations to remain in the center of the city.

2. Bed and Breakfasts - Bed and Breakfasts are a wonderful choice for those who want a more personal and home-like environment. They are often situated in neighborhood regions of Calgary.

3. Hostels - Hostels offer budget-friendly accommodations and are excellent for solitary passengers or those seeking to meet other travelers.

4. Vacation accommodations - Vacation accommodations are a wonderful choice for those seeking a more private and home-like environment.

5. Camping - For those wanting to get close to wildlife, camping is a wonderful choice. There are numerous campgrounds in the region, from RV areas to backcountry locations.

What Are Their Pay Per Night Rates?

The pay-per-night prices of accommodation in Calgary differ depending on the sort of accommodation and the location you are staying in. Generally, motels range from $50 - $200 per night, while vacation cottages can range from $50 - $500 per night. Bed and Breakfasts and lodgings are generally more inexpensive, varying from $25 - $100 per night. Camping can be more inexpensive, with per-night prices from $15 - $50.

The Names Of Considerable Accommodations, Their Locations, And Prices:

HOTELS

1. The International Hotel and Suites Calgary is located in central Calgary. Prices vary between $50 and $200 per night.

2. The Fairmont Palliser is in the center of central Calgary. Prices per night vary between $200 and $400.

3. The Hyatt Regency Calgary is located on the outskirts of downtown. Prices per night vary between $150 and $400.

4. Westin Calgary is in the center of central Calgary. Prices per night vary between $200 and $400.

5. Delta Hotels by Marriott Calgary Downtown - Located in downtown Calgary. Prices per night vary between $150 and $400.

6. Sandman Hotel & Suites Calgary South is located in the city's south. Prices vary between $50 and $200 per night.

7. Hotel Elan - Located in the city's northwest. Prices vary between $80 and $200 per night.

8. Hotel Blackfoot - Located on the city's south edge. Prices vary between $80 and $200 per night.

9. Hotel Le Germain Calgary - Located in central Calgary. Prices per night vary between $200 and $400.

10. The Hampton Inn & Suites by Hilton Calgary Airport is located on the city's east edge. Prices vary between $80 and $200 per night.

HOSTELS

1. HI Calgary City Centre - Centrally located in central Calgary. Prices vary between $25 and $50 per night.

2. The Econo Lodge midtown is in the center of midtown. Prices vary between $25 and $50 per night.

3. Hostelling International Calgary is located in the city's northwest. Prices vary between $25 and $50 per night.

4. International Youth Hostel - Located in the city's southeast. Prices vary between $25 and $50 per night.

5. The Backpackers Inn is located in the city's northwest. Prices vary between $25 and $50 per night.

6. Kensington Riverside Inn Hostel is located in the city's northwest. Prices vary between $25 and $50 per night.

7. Base Calgary is located in the city's southeast. Prices vary between $25 and $50 per night.

8. Hostel Village is located in the city's northeast. Prices vary between $25 and $50 per night.

9. Hello, Alberta Rocky Mountain House is located outside of town. Prices vary between $25 and $50 per night.

10. Luxe B&B is located in the city's northwest. Prices vary between $25 and $50 per night.

BED AND BREAKFAST

1. Kensington Riverside Inn is located in the city's northwest. Prices vary between $50 and $150 per night.

2. Luxe B&B is located in the city's northwest. Prices vary between $50 and $150 per night.

3. The Red House Bed and Breakfast is located in the city's southwest. Prices vary between $50 and $150 per night.

4. Calgary Bed & Breakfast - Located in the city's northwest. Prices vary between $50 and $150 per night.

5. The Kensington Inn is located in the city's northwest. Prices vary between $50 and $150 per night.

6. The Rose B&B is located in the city's northeast. Prices vary between $50 and $150 per night.

7. Heritage Park Bed & Breakfast is located in the city's southeast. Prices vary between $50 and $150 per night.
8. The Country Bed & Breakfast is located in the city's southeast. Prices vary between $50 and $150 per night.

9. The House of the Rising Sun Bed & Breakfast is located in the city's northwest. Prices vary between $50 and $150 per night.

10. Park Avenue Bed & Breakfast is located in the city's southwest. Prices vary between $50 and $150 per night.

VACATION RENTALS

1. The Parkview is located in the city's northeast. Prices per night vary from about $50 to $500.

2. Hillside House is located in the city's northwest. Prices per night vary from about $50 to $500.

3. Riverfront Retreat is located in the city's southeast. Prices per night vary from about $50 to $500.

4. The Cozy Cottage is located in the city's northwest. Prices per night vary from about $50 to $500.

5. Rocky Mountains Retreat - Located just outside of town. Prices per night vary from about $50 to $500.

6. midtown Loft - This loft is located in the center of midtown. Prices per night vary from about $50 to $500.

7. Luxury penthouse in the center of midtown. Prices per night vary from about $50 to $500.

8. The Hideaway is located in the city's southwest. Prices per night vary from about $50 to $500.

9. Suite on the Creek is located in the city's northwest. Prices per night vary from about $50 to $500.

10. The apartment is located in the city's northeast. Prices per night vary from about $50 to $500.

CAMPING

1. Fish Creek Provincial Park is located in the city's south. Prices vary between $15 and $50 per night.

2. Sikome Lake Campground is located in the city's southeast. Prices vary between $15 and $50 per night.

3. Silver Springs Campground is located northwest of town. Prices vary between $15 and $50 per night.

4. Pine Creek Campground is located southwest of town. Prices vary between $15 and $50 per night.

5. Bow Valley Provincial Park is located just outside of town. Prices vary between $15 and $50 per night.

6. Ghost Wilderness Campground is located just outside of town. Prices vary between $15 and $50 per night.

7. Birch Bay RV Park is located in the city's south. Prices vary between $15 and $50 per night.

8. Nose Creek Campground is located northwest of town. Prices vary between $15 and $50 per night.

9. Bow Valley Campground is located just outside of town. Prices vary between $15 and $50 per night.

10. Sundance Lodges - Sundance Lodges are located southwest of the metropolis. Prices vary between $15 and $50 per night.

My encounter with Calgary's lodging choices was excellent. I remained in motels, bed and breakfasts, dormitories, holiday accommodations, and outdoor grounds. They were all spotless, pleasant, and provided excellent service. I was able to locate lodging that met both my price and my tastes. I especially liked the bed and breakfasts and holiday accommodations because they provided a more homey ambiance. Overall, my experience with Calgary's lodging choices was very good.

My advice to anyone traveling to Calgary is to do your study and locate the best lodging for your money and tastes. There are many various kinds of accommodations in Calgary, so make sure you look into all of your choices. Also, make sure to reserve your accommodations ahead of time, as costs can rise during the busy season. Finally, enjoy Calgary's lively evening and experience everything the city has to offer.

What To Eat

Calgary has a broad culinary culture that has something for everyone. You're guaranteed to find something to your liking, from classic Canadian cooking to foreign cuisine. Here are some ideas on things to eat and drink in Calgary:

Traditional Canadian cuisine: There are a variety of restaurants in Calgary that provide traditional Canadian delicacies such as poutine, butter tarts, and Nanaimo bars. Try the poutine at La Banquise or the butter tarts at The Old Spaghetti Factory for a genuinely authentic experience.

International food: Calgary is also an excellent location for sampling international cuisine from throughout the globe. There are eateries to suit every taste, from Indian to Thai to Italian. Try the Ethiopian meal at Habesha or the Vietnamese food at Pho Hoang for a unique dining experience.

Calgary boasts a thriving nightlife culture with something for everyone. There are several venues to grab a drink and a bite to eat, ranging from quiet pubs to busy bars. Try the Calgary Tower Sky 360 Restaurant and Lounge for a one-of-a-kind experience with spectacular views of the city.

Here are a few particular ideas for Calgary restaurants and bars:

The Calgary Tower Sky 360 Restaurant and Lounge, provides amazing views of the city as well as a menu of contemporary Canadian cuisine.

La Banquise: This renowned restaurant is famed for its poutine, which consists of fresh-cut fries, cheese curds, and gravy.

The Old Spaghetti Factory: This family-friendly restaurant provides traditional Italian fare such as spaghetti & meatballs, lasagna, and fettuccine alfredo.

Habesha: With its community dining tables and delectable food, this Ethiopian restaurant provides a one-of-a-kind eating experience.

Pho Hoang: This Vietnamese restaurant is an excellent spot to taste pho, a classic Vietnamese street cuisine.

The Ship and Anchor: This historic tavern is a favorite for live music and excellent beer.

The Palomino: A country-western pub where you may dance the night away.

The National Beer Hall: This German-style beer hall serves a broad variety of beers on tap as well as a menu of classic German cuisine.

The Carousel Bar: This rotating bar provides amazing city views as well as a beverage and small plate menu.

The Beltline Brewing Company: This brewery serves a variety of artisan beers on tap as well as pub fare.

Whatever your tastes are, you're likely to find something to your liking in Calgary. Come on down and discover the city's unique food scene!

Here are a few more ideas for delicious food and drink in Calgary:

Request suggestions from locals. Calgary is a pleasant city where everyone is eager to share their favorite sites.

Examine internet reviews. Some many websites and applications may assist you in finding fantastic restaurants and pubs.

Participate in culinary festivals. Throughout the year, Calgary organizes several culinary festivals that are a terrific chance to try a range of cuisines.

Attend a culinary lesson. Many culinary schools in Calgary provide lessons for people of different skill levels.

Pay a visit to the Calgary Farmers' Market. The Calgary Farmer's Market is an excellent source of fresh fruit, meats, cheeses, and other locally produced foods.

With so many alternatives, you're bound to find something to your liking in Calgary. Come on down and discover the city's unique food scene!

Here are some more Calgary dining and drinking recommendations:

Make your bookings ahead of time. It's a good idea to make reservations in advance, particularly for popular restaurants and pubs, especially if you're going during peak season.

Use happy hour to your advantage. Happy hour promotions are available at many restaurants and pubs and may be a wonderful way to save money on beverages and food.

Experiment with something new. Don't be scared to try something new since Calgary's food culture is broad. You could perhaps discover a new favorite meal.

Expect to pay a premium. Calgary is a huge city, thus food and drink costs might be higher than in smaller places.

You'll have a terrific time dining and drinking in Calgary if you keep these suggestions in mind.

Here are some typical meal and beverage costs in Calgary:

Appetizers range between $10 and $20.

The main course costs between $20 and $30.

Dessert ranges from $10 to $15.

Beer: $5-$7

$10-$15 for a cocktail; $7-$10 for a glass of wine

What To Do

Welcome to Calgary, the vivacious and effervescent capital of Alberta, Canada! As a tourist or first-time guest, you'll be amazed at how much there is to do and see in this busy city. Calgary's vibrant amusement and cultural sites, as well as its breathtaking outdoor activities, will keep you going back for more.

Begin your stay in downtown Calgary, where you'll find fantastic eateries, museums, theaters, and retail opportunities. If you want to do something more energetic, visit the Calgary Zoo to see a variety of untamed creatures and the adjacent Calgary Tower for a stunning perspective of the city.

Calgary is a fantastic location for nature lovers. Visit the slopes of the Rocky Mountains for some of Canada's finest trekking, mountain riding, and snowboarding. For the more daring, visit Banff National Park and experience the Canadian Rockies' magnificent summits.

No trip to Calgary is complete without experiencing the city's lively entertainment. A range of musical concerts and activities are held at brand-new locations such as the Palace Theatre and the National Music Centre. Calgary is also home to some concerts and activities, including the Calgary Stampede and the Calgary Folk Music Festival.

Calgary is an excellent choice for anyone searching for a thrilling vacation. The city has something for everyone, whether you're a nature lover or a metropolitan adventurer. So, come discover Calgary and see what it has to offer!

1. Take in the Views from the Calgary Tower: For any traveler to the city, the Calgary Tower is a must-see. It is 191 meters tall and provides breathtaking 360-degree vistas of the metropolis and beyond.

2. Explore the Calgary Zoo: With over 1,000 creatures, the Calgary Zoo is a wonderful location for the complete family to explore. Spend the day visiting the various areas and learning about the zoo's varied animals.

3. Shop at the Calgary Farmers' Market: The Calgary Farmers' Market sells a wide range of fresh and local vegetables, foods, culinary products, and other items. Spend the day perusing the booths and finding the best of the city's offerings.

4. Stroll Through Prince's Island Park: Prince's Island Park is a beautiful place to get away from the rush and activity of the metropolis. Take a stroll around the island or have a meal in the park.

5. Visit the Glenbow Museum: The Glenbow Museum is one of the finest attractions in Calgary. It displays a diverse variety of artwork, relics, and exhibits from all over the globe.

6. Ski at Canada Olympic Park: For winter sports aficionados, Canada Olympic Park is the ideal location. On the hills of this world-class complex, you can ski, snowboard, and do other activities.

7. Enjoy the Calgary Stampede: Canada's biggest outdoor display and the city's hallmark event, the Calgary Stampede. Enjoy the equestrian activities, the fairground, and some of the city's finest cuisine.

8. Visit the Telus Spark Science Centre: The Telus Spark Science Centre is a hands-on science center that provides a range of engaging displays and events.

Science and technology can be learned entertainingly and interestingly!

9. Explore the Heritage Park Historical Village: The Heritage Park Historical Village is an open-air exhibit that recounts Calgary's and the neighboring area's past. Take a walk through the town and look at the ancient structures and relics.

10. Tour the Art Museum of Calgary: The Art Gallery of Calgary is Canada's biggest public art museum. Explore the gallery's remarkable selection of Canadian and foreign artwork on a guided walk.

My visit to Calgary as a visitor was remarkable. I was able to learn about the city's rich culture and history, as well as its natural beauty. I also got the opportunity to sample some of the city's delectable cuisine and wine.

The Calgary Tower was one of my favorite things to do in Calgary. The tower provides breathtaking views of the city and neighboring mountains. I loved going to the

Calgary Zoo, which has creatures from all over the globe.

If you want to do something outside, Calgary offers lots of possibilities. I went for a stroll at Fish Creek Park, which is a lovely park with several trails. I also went hiking in Kananaskis Country, a stunning mountain region just west of Calgary.

Of course, no visit to Calgary would be complete without sampling some of the city's delectable cuisine. I got the opportunity to experience poutine, a Canadian meal consisting of french fries, cheese curds, and gravy. I also got the opportunity to taste bannock, a Native American bread.

I had a fantastic experience in Calgary and would suggest it to anybody seeking a fun location to visit. Here are some of the things I did as a visitor to Calgary:
I went to the Calgary Tower.
I went to the Calgary Zoo.
I took a stroll around Fish Creek Park.

I went hiking in Kananaskis Country.

Have you tried poutine?

Have you tried Bannock?

Here are some more things to do in Calgary:

Ice skating in Olympic Plaza with GGo

Take a stroll along Stephen Avenue.

Shop at the Chinook Centre.

Snowboard or ski in Sunshine Village or Lake Louise.

Pay a visit to Banff National Park.

Ride a hot air balloon above the city.

I hope this has provided you with some ideas for things to do in Calgary!

What To Pack

Are you planning a trip to Calgary for a memorable experience? If that's the case, you'll need to make sure you're relaxed and equipped for whatever the metropolis tosses at you. Whether it's a summer road journey or a winter mountain getaway, here's a complete list of things to remember:

1. Warm and weatherproof clothing: The weather in Calgary is erratic and can change rapidly, so make sure you're equipped for whatever the factors may deliver. Pack comfortable clothing that is impermeable, such as a parka, cap, scarf, and mittens. If you're going in the winter, bring a thick winter coat and snow boots.

2. soft sneakers: Because you'll be traveling a lot, soft shoes are essential. Pack a decent set of trekking footwear if you intend to go camping or sightseeing.

3. sunblock and eyeglasses: Even if the weather forecast calls for overcast skies, it's always a good idea to bring sunblock and shades to shield yourself from the heat.

4. A compact first aid box: Your first aid bag should include a few essential things such as gauze, cleaning swabs, and pain medication.

5. If you're visiting Calgary in the spring or summer, bring a compact parasol in case of weather.

6. Camera: Don't neglect to bring a camera to record all of the incredible views and experiences you'll have in Calgary.

7. A laptop or tablet: If you'll be traveling for business or education, having a laptop or tablet with you can be extremely useful.

8. Power converter: Bring a power charger with you to keep your devices fueled.

You'll have a memorable time in Calgary if you bring these necessary things. Have fun on your journey!

Calgary has four seasons: winter, spring, summer, and autumn. Winter temps average -9°C (16°F), with snow and frigid conditions common. Spring temps average 8°C (46°F), and the days become longer and brighter. Summer temps average 22°C (72°F), with lengthy and bright days. Temperatures in the autumn average 10°C (50°F), the days become shorter, and the foliage begins to change color. Calgary is a lovely location to come to no matter what time of year you visit.

WHAT TO BRING FOR SUMMER

I brought a variety of items for my summer journey to Calgary to ensure that I was equipped for any type of weather. In case the weather was bright and balmy, I brought a light windbreaker, a sunhat, eyeglasses, and sunblock. I also brought several pieces of clothing, including a sweatshirt and a thicker overcoat, in case the weather went chilly. I packed comfy sneakers for touring the city as well as a compact parasol in case of weather. I also brought a tiny first-aid box, my laptop, a power converter, and my camera to record all of the incredible views.

WHAT TO BRING FOR WINTER

I prepared things that would keep me toasty and comfy for my winter journey to Calgary. I packed a thick winter parka, a toasty cap, scarf, and mittens, as well as a decent set of weatherproof snow boots. I also brought a few pieces of apparel - sweatshirts, thermals, and wool - to keep me toasty no matter what the weather was like. I took my camera to record the lovely views of winter in

Calgary, as well as a compact first aid box in case anything went wrong. I also packed my notebook and a power adaptor to remain linked while traveling.

WHAT TO BRING FOR SPRING

I prepared a range of things for my spring vacation to Calgary. I packed a light windbreaker and a cardigan in case the temperature fell, as well as a few pieces of apparel to accommodate shifting conditions. I also brought a small parasol in case it rained, as well as a sunhat and shades in case it was bright and balmy. I packed comfy sneakers for touring the city as well as a compact first aid box in case of minor accidents. I also packed my camera and notebook, as well as a power converter, to remain linked while traveling.

My preparation experience for my Calgary vacation was fantastic! I felt ready for whatever the weather had in store for me, and I had everything I needed to make the most of my journey. By preparing appropriately, I would make the most of my stay in Calgary and fully appreciate the city.

My advice to visitors to Calgary is to always be prepared for shifting conditions. Because Calgary can experience all four seasons in a single day, bring a range of things to help you adapt to shifting temps. Bring a few pieces of apparel as well as a weatherproof parka, cap, and mittens in case of rain. Remember to carry a sunhat and shades if the weather is bright and humid. Finally, bring a camera and a notebook with a power converter so you can remain linked while you're gone.

WHAT TO BRING FOR FALL

I prepared things that would be suitable for the shifting weather for my autumn journey to Calgary. In case the weather fell, I packed a few pieces of clothing, including a light windbreaker and a cardigan. In case the weather was bright and balmy, I also packed a sunhat and eyeglasses. I packed comfy sneakers for touring the city as well as a compact parasol in case of weather. I also brought a tiny first-aid box, my laptop, a power converter, and my camera to record all of the incredible views.

WHAT NOT TO BRING AS A TOURIST

A few things are unnecessary and should be left at home when preparing for Calgary. Heavy winter apparel (unless you're traveling in the winter), numerous mementos, and any superfluous technological devices are examples. Furthermore, you won't need to bring much currency because there are plenty of ATMs in Calgary.

There are a few things you should not carry with you when preparing for Calgary. This includes heavier winter apparel and any superfluous electrical gadgets, as Calgary sees all four seasons. Furthermore, you won't need to bring much currency because there are plenty of ATMs in Calgary. You also don't need to bring many mementos because there are plenty of excellent things available throughout the city. Finally, costly jewels or other assets should not be brought because they are easily misplaced or taken.

Tips For Exploring Calgary's Activities

1. Wear for the Weather: Calgary's weather can be quite unpredictable, so it's essential to wear appropriately for the season. If you intend to spend any time outside in the cold, pack a parka, cap, and mittens.

2. Purchase Tickets in Advance: Because many of Calgary's sites are famous, it's a good idea to purchase tickets in advance to prevent lengthy lineups.

3. Reserve excursions in preparation: If you intend to take any organized excursions, it is best to do so in preparation to guarantee access.

4. Wear easy Shoes: You'll be strolling a lot in Calgary, so wear easy shoes.

5. Plan early: With so many activities to see and do in Calgary, it's a good idea to plan early to make the most of your stay.

6. Look for Free sites: There are many free sites in Calgary, so don't neglect to look into these choices if you want to save money.

I used these suggestions while experiencing Calgary's activities by dressing appropriately for the temperature, purchasing tickets in advance, scheduling excursions in advance, wearing comfy sneakers, preparing ahead, and visiting the free sites. I was happy I had planned ahead of time and planned my activities, as it allowed me to make the most of my time in the metropolis. I also made a point of booking excursions ahead of time to guarantee access and purchasing passes ahead of time to prevent lengthy queues. I also packed a parka, cap, and mittens in case the temperature shifted. It was also essential to wear comfy sneakers because I did a lot of strolling while viewing the various sites. Finally, I made a point of visiting the complimentary sites to save money.

CHAPTER 3: GETTING TO CALGARY

Calgary is one of the most active cities in Alberta, Canada, with a plethora of attractions and activities for tourists to enjoy. There are various methods to come to Calgary, whether you're coming for business or pleasure. The fastest method to travel to Calgary International Airport is to fly.

If you prefer to travel by rail, VIA Rail provides daily service from Vancouver, Edmonton, and Winnipeg to Calgary, with multiple stops along the route. This is an excellent choice if you want a picturesque journey with lots of time to relax and enjoy the scenery. Greyhound also provides daily bus service to and from Calgary, with tickets ranging in price from $50 to $100 per person. If you want a more economical alternative, you may fly into Edmonton International Airport and then take the bus or a rental vehicle to Calgary.

Getting to Calgary, regardless of means of transportation, may be a pleasurable experience. You can determine the best route to go to this wonderful city with a little preparation and study. So begin arranging your vacation now and prepare for a wonderful trip to Calgary!

Calgary, Alberta, Canada, is a dynamic and varied city with a plethora of attractions, activities, and services that draw people from all over the globe. Some people find it difficult to get to Calgary, but with a bit of preparation and study, you can discover the best method to get to this wonderful city. Here are some of the several forms of transportation available to travel to Calgary and the cost breakdown for each conveyance to Calgary, so you can make an educated selection for your next trip.

By Plane:

Flying to Calgary is the most convenient mode of transportation. Calgary International Airport is the busiest in Alberta, with flights to and from major cities across the world. If you want to save money, travel to

Edmonton International Airport and then take the bus or rent a car to Calgary. Calgary International Airport, located about 17 kilometers northeast of the city center, offers air service. A round-trip ticket from inside Canada may cost anything from $100 to $500 depending on the time of year and how far in advance you book. A round-trip ticket from the United States might cost anywhere from $250 and $800, depending on the distance and airline.

By Car

Consider driving to Calgary if you prefer a more relaxing way of transportation. Calgary is positioned along the Trans-Canada Highway, making it approachable from all around the country. You may be able to get a rental car or plan for a ride-share based on your area. Driving to Calgary is a choice if you're coming from Alberta or a close state. Depending on where you start, gas will cost between $60 and $80 for a round-trip from Edmonton and between $140 and $180 from Vancouver. Keep in mind that if you want to drive into downtown Calgary, you'll also need to prepare for parking costs.

By Train,

The cost of riding a train to get to Calgary depends vary on your starting location and the type of service you pick. VIA Rail, the national passenger rail service in Canada, provides train service to Calgary from Vancouver and Toronto.

If you're flying from Vancouver, the cost of a one-way ticket to Calgary may start at roughly CAD 200 for Economy class, CAD 300 for Business class, and CAD 600 for Sleeper class.

If you're coming from Toronto, the cost of a one-way ticket to Calgary may start at roughly CAD 300 for Economy class, CAD 560 for Business class, and CAD 1,100 for Sleeper class.

It's crucial to remember that rates might vary based on the time of year, how far in advance you purchase your ticket, and whether you pick a flexible or non-flexible fare. VIA Rail provides numerous discounts and promotions throughout the year, so it's always a good idea to check their website for the newest specials.

Overall, traveling by rail to Calgary may be a pleasant and picturesque way to travel, but it may be more costly than other forms of transportation such as bus or automobile. It's crucial to consider your budget and travel preferences when determining which method of transportation to use.

By Bus

If you want to get to Calgary for less money, think about using the bus. From Vancouver, Edmonton, and Winnipeg as well as several other places along the road, Greyhound runs daily service to Calgary. Even while the trip may take longer than flying or taking the train, it's a great way to see the country while saving money. No of the method of transportation, getting to Calgary might be an amazing event. With a little planning and study, you may choose the best way to take to reach this beautiful city. Bus travel to Calgary is an inexpensive choice if you're going from a nearby city or town. Prices for one-way trips to Calgary with Greyhound and Red Arrow start at around $30 from different places in Alberta and Saskatchewan. Expect to spend between $50 and $80 for a one-way ticket if you're going from Vancouver or Edmonton.

To go to Calgary, I took a combination of an aircraft and a vehicle. To get to my destination, I flew into Calgary International Airport and then hired a vehicle. My journey to Calgary was fantastic. The journey was uneventful, and renting a vehicle was simple. I had plenty of time to enjoy the landscape along the route, and it was stunning. I was able to get to Calgary quickly.

To sum up, the cost of each journey to Calgary varies based on the form of transportation and your starting point. When deciding which method of transportation is best for you on your next trip to Calgary, take your budget, journey time, and convenience into account. You may select a mode of transportation that suits your requirements and your budget thanks to the wide range of alternatives available.

CHAPTER 4: GETTING AROUND CALGARY

The city's excellent transit infrastructure makes getting about Calgary as a visitor a snap. Here are some helpful hints for navigating Calgary, including transit alternatives and estimated costs per trip:

Calgary Transit (Bus and CTrain): Calgary Transit maintains a comprehensive bus and CTrain (light rail) network that serves the whole city and its neighboring regions. Buses and CTrains are an inexpensive and handy method to get to Calgary. A single adult ticket costs around CAD 3.50 and allows for unlimited transfers within a 90-minute window.

Taxis and ridesharing Services: Taxis are widely accessible in Calgary, while ridesharing services such as Uber and Lyft are also available. Taxis and ridesharing services provide quick door-to-door transportation. Taxi costs begin from CAD 3.80, with extra charges for each kilometer or minute. Fares for ridesharing vary according to distance and demand.

Automobile Rentals: If you prefer the freedom of owning a vehicle, automobile rentals are available at the Calgary International Airport and numerous rental firms across the city. Prices vary according to the rental business, car type, and rental term. It is best to reserve ahead of time and check for any extra expenses, such as insurance and gasoline taxes.

Bike Rentals and Pathways: Calgary has a vast network of bike routes and lanes, making it an excellent destination for cyclists. Several bike rental establishments provide hourly, daily, and weekly rentals. Prices vary from CAD 8-15 per hour or CAD 25-40 per day. Cycling throughout the city enables you to explore at your leisure while taking in the city's gorgeous parks and walkways.

Walking: The downtown center of Calgary is pedestrian-friendly, with numerous attractions, shops, and restaurants within walking distance. Exploring by foot enables you to immerse yourself in the dynamic ambiance of the city while also discovering hidden jewels along the route. Walking is, of course, free and provides a distinct viewpoint of the city.

As a practical tip, organize your transportation alternatives depending on your schedule and the distance between sites. The city's small structure, along with Calgary's integrated transit system, makes it simple to traverse and explore. Based on your unique requirements and interests, consider combining public transit, walking, and other choices.

Please keep in mind that the prices shown are estimates and subject to change. For the most up-to-date information on rates, timetables, and routes, it is always best to visit official websites or speak with transportation providers.

CHAPTER 5: EXPLORING CALGARY

Exploring Calgary as a visitor provides a wealth of practical experiences that will fascinate you with the city's allure. Here are some great sites to visit and helpful hints for your adventure:

Calgary Tower

For a bird's-eye perspective of the city, visit the Calgary Tower. Take the glass elevator to the observation deck for 360-degree views of downtown Calgary and the surrounding surroundings. Visit around sunset to view the amazing splendor of the city lights illuminating the skyline.

Calgary Zoo

Take an adventurous tour around the Calgary Zoo, which is home to a wide variety of species from across the globe. Come up close and personal with giraffes, penguins, and gorillas. Don't miss out on the immersive ecosystems, such as the Penguin Plunge and the Canadian Wilds, where you may witness native Canadian creatures in their natural habitats.

Heritage Park Historical Village

An immersive living history museum, Heritage Park Historical Village transports visitors back in time. Explore historic structures, ride a vintage steam train, and engage with costumed interpreters who bring the past to life. Don't forget to stop by the bakery and ice cream shop for some old-fashioned delights.

Fish Creek Provincial Park:

Visit Fish Creek Provincial Park to get away from the rush and bustle of the city. This urban paradise is ideal for hiking, bicycling, and picnics, with over 80 kilometers of pathways. Explore the winding paths, take in the picturesque vistas of the Bow River, and keep a lookout for local animals such as deer and birds.

Glenbow Museum

At the Glenbow Museum, you may immerse yourself in art, culture, and history. Discover the many exhibitions that highlight Western Canadian art, indigenous heritage, and foreign cultures. The museum provides a thorough look at the region's legacy, ranging from current art to ancient antiquities.

Stephen Avenue Walk

Take a leisurely walk around downtown Calgary's pedestrian-friendly Stephen Avenue Walk. Explore a diverse range of stores, restaurants, cafés, and entertainment places. Browse stores, get a cup of coffee at a local café, and take in street performances and live music.

Canada Olympic Park

Relive the excitement of the 1988 Winter Olympics at Canada Olympic Park. Ski or snowboard on the slopes throughout the winter. Try your hand at adrenaline-pumping sports like ziplining, mountain biking, or a trip on North America's fastest zipline throughout the summer.

Calgary Farmers' Market

The Calgary Farmer's Market is a sensory treat. Taste fresh vegetables, regional specialties, artisanal items, and handcrafted crafts. Interact with local merchants, consume wonderful sweets, and enjoy the lively environment.

Before you go, double-check the operation hours and any required reservations or tickets for each attraction. The practical experiences in Calgary provide a broad choice of encounters that enable you to immerse yourself in the city's culture, history, and natural beauty. So put on your sneakers, grab your camera, and set off on a thrilling adventure across Calgary's greatest attractions.

CHAPTER 6: SHOPPING AND MALL

As a visitor in Calgary, Canada, I engaged in a retail excursion that left an unforgettable impact on my shopping experience. Calgary's retail culture provides a compelling combination of experiences for every tourist, from sophisticated malls to quaint shops and local markets. Join me as I discuss my own experience and provide practical ideas for making the most of your shopping trip in Calgary.

Stephen Avenue Walk and The CORE Shopping Centre in Downtown Calgary: My retail adventure started in downtown Calgary, where I was instantly drawn to the vibrancy of Stephen Avenue Walk. The pedestrian-only boulevard was a haven for stores, boutiques, and cafés, each of which provided a distinct peek into Calgary's diverse culture. Stephen Avenue Walk presented a treasure trove of unique treasures that wonderfully embodied the heart of my vacation, from locally produced souvenirs to modern fashion businesses.

I found The CORE Shopping Centre, a magnificent shopping oasis in the middle of the city, next to this busy street. Entering The CORE was like stepping into a realm of luxury and grandeur. The high-end fashion stores featured the newest trends and designer collections from recognized names such as Gucci, Louis Vuitton, and Burberry. My shopping experience was boosted by the attentive service and elegant ambiance, making it a memorable highlight of my vacation.

Chinook Centre is a shopping paradise: My shopping adventure in Calgary took me to Chinook Centre, the city's biggest mall. Chinook Centre provided an unrivaled shopping experience with over 250 retailers. I noticed a large assortment of apparel, accessories, cosmetic goods, and home décor as I walked around the mall. Chinook Centre caters to every style and inclination, from globally famous companies like Zara and H&M to traditional department shops like Hudson's

Bay. I relished a fantastic dinner at one of the mall's numerous eating choices, which spanned from fast-casual eateries to fancy restaurants, after indulging in retail therapy.

CrossIron Mills: A Shopping Paradise Just outside of town, I discovered CrossIron Mills, an outlet mall that quickly became a shopaholic's dream. CrossIron Mills had an alluring charm with over 200 retailers providing discounts on designer brands, home furnishings, recreational goods, and more. I got great savings on popular brands like Nike, Coach, and Calvin Klein, and I loved the excitement of discovering hidden gems at rock-bottom rates. The mall's inviting ambiance and many eating selections offered the ideal relaxation after a day of shopping.

Inglewood is a haven for one-of-a-kind finds: I went to Inglewood, Calgary's oldest area, to add some local flavor to my shopping experience. The streets were dotted with beautiful hippie shops, art galleries, and antique stores. I became engaged in the creative atmosphere and found one-of-a-kind objects made by local craftsmen. From handcrafted jewelry and antique apparel to one-of-a-kind home décor products, Inglewood provided a unique shopping experience. I loved the warmth and character of the area as I sipped a cup of coffee at a comfortable café and dined at one of the neighborhood's charming eateries.

Practical Advice for a Memorable Shopping Experience:

Transportation: For easy transit between shopping sites, take advantage of Calgary's excellent public transportation system or explore ridesharing services. To maximize your time, plan your routes and keep an eye out for any timetable changes.

Money: As a visitor, having Canadian money for cash purchases is advantageous since certain smaller vendors and marketplaces may not take credit cards. Learn about current exchange rates and consider exchanging money ahead of time.

Tax Refunds: Tourists may take advantage of tax refund schemes on specific purchases. To save money, look for eligible shops and enquire about the tax refund procedure.

Engage with Local Markets: Explore the local farmers' markets and craft fairs to immerse yourself in Calgary's colorful culture. For a genuine experience, sample great local vegetables, artisan handicrafts, and connect with friendly merchants.

Shopping Etiquette: Follow store regulations, ask for help when required, and be kind to other customers. Engage in discussions with shop employees, who are typically ready to provide product ideas and insights.

Conclusion:

My shopping adventure across Calgary's malls and shopping pleasures was an enthralling mix of luxury, local charm, and one-of-a-kind bargains. Each encounter, from the busy streets of downtown Calgary to the enormous malls and quaint shops, brought a layer of depth to my journey. With these practical recommendations in mind, appreciate Calgary's shopping enchantment, immersing yourself in a world of fashion, local treasures, and gastronomic pleasures. Allow Calgary's retail scene to pique your curiosity and create amazing moments that you will remember long after your visit.

Popular Shopping District

Here is a list of Calgary's popular shopping venues, their locations, and some popular things available:

Stephen Avenue Stroll:

Calgary's downtown core

Popular items include local artisan crafts, fashion boutiques, one-of-a-kind souvenirs, and specialized shops.

CORE Shopping Center:

Calgary's downtown core

High-end fashion companies, premium accessories, designer collections, and posh department shops are popular.

The Chinook Centre:

Location: South of Calgary's downtown.

Fashion clothes, cosmetic goods, home décor, technology, and a broad range of eating alternatives are all popular items.

Mills, CrossIron:

Location: Just outside of town

Popular items include discounted designer labels, home furnishings, sports goods, technology, and broad restaurant choices.

Inglewood:

The oldest neighborhood in Calgary

Popular goods include handmade jewelry, vintage apparel, one-of-a-kind home décor, local art, and a variety of diverse eating experiences.

17th Avenue SW, sometimes known as the "Red Mile," is a vibrant corridor full of stylish shops, fashion-forward retailers, and sophisticated eateries. It is a fashion enthusiast's paradise, with a vast selection of apparel, accessories, and home décor.

Kensington Village: Kensington Village, located in Calgary's northwest quarter, is a quaint and diverse community recognized for its bohemian attitude. The neighborhood is densely packed with boutique retailers, independent booksellers, vintage apparel stores, and specialty food stores. It's a terrific location to locate one-of-a-kind products.

Chinatown: Chinatown in Calgary, situated near the downtown center, provides a culturally rich retail experience. The neighborhood is well-known for its Asian grocers, herbal medicine stores, and genuine Asian eateries. Visitors may peruse the colorful markets for one-of-a-kind ingredients, traditional Chinese teas, and other Asian-inspired items.

These famous Calgary retail areas provide a wide variety of shopping experiences, from high-end fashion to antique treasures and one-of-a-kind local discoveries. Each district has its distinct personality and ambiance, ensuring that consumers have a pleasurable and stimulating shopping experience also keep in mind that particular item availability varies depending on individual shops within these shopping places. It is usually best to visit the businesses in person or check their websites for a complete list of items.

No-Tax Shopping

Most products and services are exempt from provincial sales tax (PST) or provincial value-added tax (VAT) in Calgary and across Alberta. This means that when you purchase in Calgary, you may benefit from tax-free shopping, which can result in big savings.

Calgary's lack of a provincial sales tax makes it an appealing shopping destination for both residents and tourists. It indicates that the price on the tag is the amount you pay at the checkout counter, less any extra taxes. This simple pricing method streamlines the shopping experience and provides you with a clear idea of the cost of your products.

No-tax shopping in Calgary may result in significant savings, particularly on high-priced products. Because there is no provincial sales tax, the ultimate cost of an item may be much cheaper than in provinces or countries where sales taxes are levied.

While there is no provincial sales tax in Calgary, there are still federal charges to be aware of, such as the Goods and Services Tax (GST), which is presently set at 5%. This federal tax applies to the majority of products and services bought in Canada, including those purchased in Calgary. Even with the GST, the total tax burden in Calgary is lower than in other jurisdictions with extra sales taxes.

No-tax shopping in Calgary allows you to stretch your money and maybe indulge in more shopping or higher-value goods, enabling you to stretch your budget further. Whether you're looking for apparel, electronics, household products, or other things, the lack of provincial sales tax in Calgary makes shopping more reasonable and appealing.

It's vital to remember that tax rules may change over time, and it's always a good idea to remain up to speed on any adjustments or revisions to the tax system. Furthermore, some products and services may still be subject to special taxes or levies, so check with individual stores or the Canadian Revenue Agency for more details.

To summarize, the no-tax shopping experience in Calgary is a significant benefit that distinguishes the city as a popular shopping destination. Because there is no provincial sales tax, customers may enjoy straightforward pricing and possible savings, making their shopping experience in Calgary even more delightful.

Bargaining Tips

When visiting Calgary as a tourist, knowing how to haggle will help you obtain the greatest discounts and pricing. Here are some negotiation strategies to remember throughout your visit:

Research and Compare pricing: Before engaging in any negotiating, research to obtain an understanding of the usual pricing for products and services in Calgary. Compare pricing at several vendors or places to get a sense of what you should anticipate spending.

Begin with Polite Negotiation: Approach negotiation circumstances warmly and politely. Engage the vendor or seller in a discussion, demonstrating your interest in their goods or service. "Is there any room for negotiation on the price?" or "Would you consider offering a discount?"

Bundle or Buy in quantity: Consider combining numerous things or buying in quantity to negotiate a lower price. When a vendor sees the possibility of a greater transaction, he or she may be more ready to provide a discount.

Be Aware of Cultural Sensitivities: Bargaining is a widespread activity in certain cultures, but it may be less so in others. Negotiating pricing at markets, street sellers, or small stores is often accepted in Calgary. However, negotiating may not be as prevalent or well-received in bigger retail establishments or established firms. Consider the situation and adjust your approach appropriately.

Maintain a Reasonable and Realistic Offer: Be reasonable and thoughtful while making a first counteroffer. Offering a very low price may irritate the seller and stymie any prospective discussion. Begin with an offer that is somewhat lower than the quoted price and work your way up if required.

Demonstrate real Interest: Show real interest in the product or service, emphasizing any good traits or unique aspects. This may help you build a deeper relationship with the seller and increase your chances of getting a better offer.

Consider Timing: Timing may influence negotiation success. Vendors may be more inclined to negotiate a deal towards the end of the day or during slower hours. Furthermore, if a dealer offers numerous identical things, their price may be more flexible.

Know When to Walk Away: Despite your best efforts, sometimes a mutually agreed price cannot be achieved. In such instances, knowing when to move away and consider alternative possibilities is critical. If the conditions aren't advantageous to you, don't feel forced to buy.

Remember to approach negotiations with respect and understanding. Enjoy the experience, enjoy the cultural nuances of negotiating in Calgary, and have a nice and courteous manner at all times.

CHAPTER 7: NIGHTLIFE IN CALGARY

Calgary's nightlife culture is active and diversified, catering to a broad variety of interests and inclinations. As a Calgary resident, I've had the pleasure of exploring the city's nightlife and experiencing its distinct vibe firsthand. Allow me to share some of my own experiences and ideas with you.

Calgary comes alive with energy and enthusiasm as the sun sets. For those looking for a spectacular night out, the city has several possibilities. Calgary offers it all, whether you're searching for a comfortable pub, a fashionable bar, or lively nightlife.

One of my favorite nightlife spots in Calgary is 17th Avenue SW, often known as the "Red Mile." This busy boulevard is lined with a variety of restaurants, pubs, and clubs, resulting in a lively and bustling ambiance. The Red Mile is a hive of activity, particularly on weekends and at special events when residents and tourists alike congregate to interact and enjoy the lively atmosphere.

On 17th Avenue SW, you'll discover a diverse range of restaurants catering to various preferences. There's something for everyone, from laid-back pubs and sports bars where you can watch the game with pals to upmarket clubs offering handmade drinks and live music performances. Many great hours have been spent hopping between places, sampling different beverages, and immersing myself in the bustling environment.

If you like live music, Calgary has various locations where you may see outstanding local and international acts. The National Music Centre in the East Village is a must-see for music lovers. This famous facility features concerts, exhibits, and interactive experiences commemorating music's rich history and progress. It's a fantastic spot to see a live event and immerse yourself in the enthralling world of music.

Calgary has several charming bars and speakeasies for people who want a more personal atmosphere. These hidden treasures provide an environment of exclusivity and elegance, with professional mixologists creating one-of-a-kind and artistic drinks. I've spent many enjoyable nights in these businesses, sipping excellent cocktails and conversing with friends and other customers.

Calgary's nightlife is not confined to a single neighborhood. Another dynamic attraction for those looking for a fantastic night out is the city's downtown center. There's a mix of stylish clubs, rooftop bars with spectacular views, and active dance floors where you can let free and dance the night away. The variety of alternatives means that there is always something for everyone, no matter what sort of nightlife you enjoy.

As with any evening event, being safe and drinking sensibly is essential. Calgary features dependable transportation options, such as taxis and ride-sharing applications, to guarantee you can easily get to and from your locations.

To summarize, Calgary's nightlife is active and thrilling, which I have truly enjoyed as a resident. There's a location to fit every mood and choice, from vibrant streets packed with pubs and restaurants to small salons and intense dance floors. Calgary's nightlife culture provides something for everyone, whether you're searching for a quiet evening with friends or a night of dancing and live music. So gather your pals, visit the city, and be enchanted by Calgary's nightlife.

Popular Bar and Clubs

Calgary has a vibrant and booming bar and club scene, with a wide choice of alternatives for those looking for an amazing night out. Calgary offers a location to fit your taste, whether it's a quaint neighborhood pub, a fashionable cocktail bar, or a throbbing nightclub. Let's have a look at some of the city's most popular pubs and clubs:

Commonwealth Bar and Stage is a two-story establishment that specializes in live music and DJs. It is in the center of the Beltline neighborhood. The first floor is a more casual environment with a bar, lounge seats, and a live music stage. The second level has a dance floor with a more dynamic vibe. Commonwealth Bar & Stage features a wide range of local and traveling musicians, from new bands to experienced performances. They also offer a complete bar with a food and drink menu. In addition, the lower level provides a more intimate atmosphere with a capacity of 200 people, and the top level has a larger dance floor with a capacity of 500 people.

Broken City is a well-known venue for live music and beverages. It is in the East Village neighborhood. Broken City features a huge stage in the rear of the pub where live music performances range from rock and indie to blues and jazz. There is also a complete bar with an emphasis on artisan drinks. Broken City's environment is easygoing and hospitable, making it ideal for a night out with friends. The 250-person capacity facility features a range of local and traveling performers.

The Hifi Club is a tiny and intimate venue specializing in electronic music. It's in the Mission neighborhood. With a capacity of just 200 people, the Hifi Club provides an extremely intimate and up-close experience for enthusiasts of electronic music. The Hifi Club has a range of local and international DJs, and the sound system is excellent. The Hifi Club is the place to go if you want to dance the night away to some electronic tunes.

Milk Tiger Lounge is a hip bar that specializes in specialty drinks. It's in the Beltline neighborhood. The Milk Tiger Lounge features a clean and contemporary interior design, and the drinks are inventive and excellent. They also provide charcuterie boards and cheese platters on their limited menu. Milk Tiger Lounge is an excellent choice for a stylish setting to spend a night out with friends. The lounge seats 100 people and serves handmade drinks as well as a range of local beers and wines.

Cowboys Nightclub is a huge dance club that specializes in country music. It's in the Southeast neighborhood. Cowboys Nightclub is a renowned destination for country music aficionados, hosting a range of live music performances by local and traveling musicians. A huge dance floor and a full bar are also available. Cowboys Nightclub is the place to go if you want to let free and dance the night away to some country music. The club holds 1,500 people and boasts a wide dance floor, a mechanical bull, and a VIP section.

Please Don't Tell is a members-only lounge that specializes in drinks and live music. It is in the Downtown West neighborhood. Please Don't Tell is a Calgary hidden treasure only accessible via a secret entrance in an alleyway. The pub boasts a speakeasy ambiance and some of the greatest drinks in town. They also showcase live music performances ranging from jazz to blues to rock. Please Don't Tell is the place to go if you want a one-of-a-kind and private nightlife experience. The pub has a seating capacity of 50 people and a speakeasy-style ambiance.

Ace Nightclub is a major dance club that specializes in hip-hop and electronic music. It is in the Downtown West neighborhood. The Ace Nightclub attracts individuals of all ages and has a range of live music events and DJs. A huge dance floor and a full bar are also available. If you want to dance the night away to hip-hop or electronic music, The Ace Nightclub is the place to be. The club seats 1,500 people and includes a spacious dance floor, VIP section, and rooftop terrace.

Dickens Bar is a classic British bar that specializes in beer and live music. It's in the Beltline neighborhood. Dickens Pub offers a warm and welcoming ambiance, and the beer selection is excellent. They also showcase live music performances ranging from folk to rock to blues. Dickens Pub is the ideal location to enjoy a pint of beer and some live music. The bar seats 200 people and offers a large range of beers on tap as well as a pub food menu.

The Ship & Anchor is a well-known venue for live music and artisan beer. It is in the Inglewood neighborhood. The Ship & Anchor offers a big outside terrace that is ideal for enjoying a summer night. They also serve a broad range of specialty beers on tap and have live music performances ranging from rock to blues to folk. If you want to enjoy a refreshing drink and some live music, The Ship & Anchor is the place to go. The bar seats 300 people and offers a large range of craft beers on tap as well as a pub food menu.

These are just a handful of Calgary's numerous clubs and pubs. There is something for everyone, regardless of musical or atmospheric preferences.

Tips for Staying Safe While At Night-life

When enjoying Calgary's dynamic nightlife, it's critical to prioritize your safety to guarantee a pleasant and worry-free time. Based on my experience, here are some suggestions for being safe while enjoying Calgary's nightlife:

Plan ahead of time: Before you go, acquaint yourself with the location you'll be visiting. Plan your itinerary by researching popular bars and clubs. Inform someone you trust about your intentions, including where you want to go and when you anticipate returning.

Be mindful of your surroundings: Avoid walking alone, particularly in dark or isolated regions. If you must go alone, keep your phone in hand and be mindful of your surroundings.

Don't leave your beverages unattended: this is a popular method for individuals to get intoxicated. If you need to use the restroom, take your drink with you or ask a buddy to keep an eye on it for you.

Accepting beverages from strangers is not acceptable: Even if the drink seems to be unopened, it may have been tampered with. Stick to beverages you order and observe being served for yourself.

Travel in a group of friends: This is the greatest method to be safe because you can keep an eye out for each other. If you are heading to a club or pub by yourself, inform someone of your plans and when you anticipate returning.

Trust your instincts: If someone makes you feel uneasy, don't be afraid to walk away. You owe no one an explanation.

Know your drinking limits: Don't consume excessive amounts of alcohol. The more inebriated you are, the more likely it is that you will become a victim of a crime.

Make a strategy to go home: If you're drinking, make sure you have a designated driver or a transport home scheduled.

Keep an eye on your surroundings: Take notice of who is around you and what is going on. If you see something odd, notify a security guard or bartender.

Don't flaunt your cash or valuables: this attracts criminals.

Leave if you feel unsafe: Don't be frightened to walk away from any scenario causing you unsettling.

Take a cab or ride-sharing service home: Do not walk home alone, particularly at night.

Any suspicious action should be reported to a security guard or bartender: Don't be scared to speak out if you witness someone being harassed or abused.

The workers at the bar or club are there to assist you in remaining safe.

Know Your Emergency Contacts: Make a list of emergency contact numbers, such as local police enforcement and medical agencies, and keep it on your phone. Knowing who to contact in an emergency might assist in quickly alleviating the problem. Also, if you believe you are being followed, go somewhere public or contact the police.

Above all else, follow your instincts and prioritize your safety. If anything seems odd or unpleasant, don't be afraid to leave the scene or seek help from venue employees or authorities.

You can assure a safe and pleasurable nighttime experience in Calgary by following these practical guidelines. Remember that keeping attentive, responsible, and prepared can help you have a wonderful night out while prioritizing your safety.

CHAPTER 8: EVENTS AND FESTIVALS IN CALGARY

Calgary celebrates a diverse range of events and festivals throughout the year, providing something for everyone to enjoy. From cultural festivities to music festivals, here are a few notable events, along with ticket prices and dates:

The Calgary Stampede is the city's most renowned event, occurring each July. A rodeo, chuckwagon races, music, and a midway with rides and games are all part of the 10-day celebration. Adult general admission tickets are $19, kids (6-12) tickets are $12, and children 5 and under are free. VIP seats start at $129 and go up from there.

GlobalFest is an annual international event that celebrates the variety of Calgary. It takes place in August and includes pavilions from more than 30 nations, as well as entertainment, cuisine, and fireworks. Adult general admission tickets are $15, youth (6-12) tickets are $10, and children 5 and under are free. VIP tickets start at $40 and go up from there.

Sled Island is a yearly music event that showcases independent music from all around the globe. It takes place in June at over 30 sites across the city. Single-day tickets begin at $45, while three-day packages begin at $129.

The Calgary Folk Music event is an annual folk music event that showcases both Canadian and foreign performers. It takes place in July and is hosted in Fort Calgary. Single-day tickets begin at $59, while three-day passes begin at $149.

Taste of Calgary is a culinary event that takes place every year and comprises sampling from over 100 Calgary restaurants. It takes place in downtown Calgary and is hosted every July. Adult general admission tickets are $15, youth (6-12) tickets are $10, and children 5 and under are free. VIP seats, which begin at $45, are also available.

Here are some additional important Calgary events and festivals, along with their ticket prices and dates:

General admission tickets for the Calgary International Film Festival (September) start at $12.

Single tickets for the Calgary International Comedy Festival (March) start at $25.

Single-day tickets for the Calgary Comic & Entertainment Expo (April) start at $30.

Registration for the Calgary Marathon (June) begins at $125.

Single tickets for the Calgary Fringe Festival (September) start at $10.

Please keep in mind that these are just a handful of the numerous events and festivals held in Calgary throughout the year. Please check the websites of the individual events or festivals for further information.

In 2022, I attended the Calgary Stampede. I had always wanted to attend, and now I had the opportunity. I purchased my tickets ahead of time and arrived at the Stampede grounds early in the morning.

The very first thing I did was go to the midway. There were so many rides and games that I couldn't help but try them all. I rode the Ferris wheel, roller coaster, and bumper cars. I also played some ring toss and skeeball.

I went to the rodeo after I'd gotten my fill of the midway. I had never attended a rodeo before and was astounded by the cowboys' and cowgirls' abilities. I observed them as they rode bulls, roped calves, and competed in other competitions.

In the evening, I went to the Stampede grounds to catch a concert. Many concerts were going on that day, and I was selected to attend a country music event. I had a great time at the event and danced the night away.

The Calgary Stampede was a blast for me. It was a genuinely unique experience that I would strongly suggest to anybody seeking a fun and interesting event to attend.

Here are some more specifics regarding my experience:

- My pals and I went to the Stampede. We all had a terrific time and created some new memories that we will treasure for the rest of our lives.
- We got to the Stampede grounds early in the morning to avoid the throng. This was a wise option since the grounds were quite busy later in the day.

- The midway was where we spent most of our time. We went on several rides, played some games, and ate some delectable cuisine.
- We also attended the rodeo. This was a highlight of our vacation, and we were all impressed with the cowboys' and cowgirls' abilities.
- We finished the evening with a performance at the Stampede grounds. We went to a country music event and danced all night.

Vital Tips for Enjoying Calgary's Events and Festivals.

Here are some pointers if you want to go to the Calgary Stampede:

- Purchase your tickets in advance, particularly if you want to go on a weekend.
- Wear comfy shoes since you will be walking a lot.

- Bring sunscreen and a hat since Calgary can become rather hot in July.

  .

- Be prepared for large crowds. Because the Stampede is such a popular event, it may become congested at times.

Have a good time! The Stampede is an excellent opportunity to learn about Calgary's culture and history.

CHAPTER 9: FAMILY-FRIENDLY ACTIVITIES IN CALGARY

Having personally explored the family-friendly activities in Calgary, I can share practical experiences of these wonderful attractions that provide enjoyment for the whole family. Here are some family-friendly activities in Calgary, along with their locations and ticket fees:

Calgary Zoo: The Calgary Zoo, located near Bridgeland, provides an immersive animal experience. The zoo has creatures from all over the world, from the African Savannah to the Canadian Wilds. Ticket prices vary according to season and age group. Adult general admission prices vary from $19.95 to $29.95, while children's prices range from $9.95 to $19.95, with savings available for online orders.

Telus Spark Scientific Centre: Telus Spark Science Centre, located in the Nose Creek Valley, is a center of interactive scientific displays and educational activities. Visitors may tour several galleries, engage in hands-on for activities, and learn about scientific ideas. Adult admission rates normally vary from $19.95 to $26.95, while children's admission fees range from $12.95 to $19.95.

Heritage Park Historical Village: Heritage Park Historical Village, located in Southwest Calgary, is a living history museum that provides an insight into Western Canada's past. Visitors may explore historical structures, ride a vintage steam train, and engage with costumed interpreters. Adult admission rates vary from $12.95 to $26.50, while children's admission fees range from $8.75 to $18.75, with extra expenses for train rides and activities.

Calgary Corn Maze & Enjoyment Farm: Located in southeast Calgary, the Calgary Corn Maze & Fun Farm offers outdoor family enjoyment. Activities include traversing a corn maze, taking tractor-pulled wagon rides, and participating in a variety of farm-themed activities. Ticket prices vary from $14.95 to $19.95 per person, with discounts available for seniors and children under the age of three.

Fish Creek Provincial Park: Located on the city's southern outskirts, Fish Creek Provincial Park provides abundant natural beauty and recreational activities. Hiking and bike routes, picnics along the Bow River, and animal viewing are all available to families. The park is free to enter, while certain amenities and activities may charge a fee.

These Calgary family-friendly activities provide enjoyable experiences as well as the opportunity to spend quality time with loved ones. Each site provides a unique experience for the whole family, from learning about animals at the zoo to studying scientific ideas at the Telus Spark Scientific Centre. These activities guarantee that families can build lasting memories while enjoying the finest of Calgary's family-friendly attractions, thanks to their diverse ticket prices and convenient locations.

Applicable Tips For Family-Friendly Activities

When looking for family-friendly activities in Calgary, it's important to prepare ahead of time to make the most of your time together. Here are some pointers to help you have a pleasant and pleasurable experience:

Research and Select Age-Appropriate Activities: Look for activities that are appropriate for your family members' ages and interests. Consider each attraction's suggested age limitations, height constraints, and interactive components to ensure that everyone can fully engage and have a good time.

Check Operating Hours and Availability: Before you leave, double-check the hours of operation for the attractions you want to visit. Some venues may have seasonal hours or close on certain days. Check for any special events, exhibits, or limited-time offers to enhance your experience.

Purchase Tickets in Advance: Whenever feasible, try getting tickets in advance to prevent long lines and potential disappointment. Many attractions have online tickets, enabling you to reserve your access ahead of time and maybe bypass the ticketing lineups.

Pack Essential Supplies: Bring sunscreen, water bottles, snacks, and comfortable attire depending on the activities and length of your excursion. It's also a good idea to have a small backpack or bag to transport these goods.

Follow Safety requirements: Follow any regulations or directions given by the employees, as well as any safety requirements issued by the venues, such as height and age limitations. Encourage youngsters to practice appropriate hand hygiene and to remain with the group or inside designated zones for their safety.

Participate in Educational Activities: Many family-friendly activities in Calgary have educational components. Encourage your children to participate actively, ask questions, and interact with the exhibits or displays. Take advantage of chances to study and pique your interest.

Plan for pauses and pace yourself during the day, particularly for smaller children who may need rest or food breaks. Pace your activities to keep everyone enthusiastic and involved without becoming overwhelmed or exhausted.

Capture the Moments: Bring a camera or smartphone to record special moments with your family. Documenting the event enables you to reflect on these wonderful occasions together in the future and share the memories.

Be Flexible: While having a plan is important, be open to spontaneous moments and unexpected discoveries.

Make space in your agenda for flexibility, enabling your family to explore, play, and immerse themselves in the experience.

Above all, keep in mind that the objective of family-friendly activities is to spend quality time together. Accept the chance to connect, laugh, and make memories with your loved ones. To make the most of your stay in Calgary, encourage open conversation and shared experiences.

Following these guidelines will help you navigate Calgary's family-friendly activities with ease, providing a memorable and pleasurable time for everyone in your family.

CHAPTER 10: TRAVEL INSURANCE

Obtaining travel insurance as a tourist visiting Calgary is a powerful and practical move to assure a worry-free and joyful vacation. Travel insurance is also recommended. This is because Calgary is a large city with a lot of traffic and crime.

Any traveler visiting Calgary, Alberta, should have travel insurance. The city has a chilly climate and is prone to major weather occurrences like blizzards and floods. There is also the possibility of severe weather, such as snowstorms and hailstorms.

Benefits of Travel Insurance

Here's a look at how having travel insurance in Calgary performs in application:

Peace of Mind: Having travel insurance gives you peace of mind since it protects you against unforeseen incidents that may ruin your vacation plans. Travel insurance provides a safety net, relieving financial stress and enabling you to concentrate on enjoying your stay in Calgary.

Emergency Medical Coverage: Emergency medical coverage is one of the most important features of travel insurance. Although Calgary offers great healthcare facilities, medical costs may be high, particularly for tourists. You have access to emergency medical services with travel insurance, including hospitalization, doctor consultations, and emergency medical evacuation if necessary. This coverage guarantees that you obtain the essential treatment without having to worry about the cost.

Emergency Cash Transfer: If your wallet or credit cards are lost or stolen, this service will give you cash.

Trip Cancellation & Interruption: Travel arrangements sometimes alter suddenly owing to a variety of factors such as personal crises, natural catastrophes, or unforeseeable circumstances. Travel insurance protects you financially by reimbursing non-refundable charges if your vacation is canceled or cut short. This coverage enables you to postpone or prepare an alternate trip without incurring the entire cost load.

Baggage Misplaced or Delayed: Imagine landing in Calgary only to discover that your baggage has been misplaced or delayed. You may be compensated for the necessary products you need to buy while your luggage is being found if you have travel insurance. Because you will be reimbursed for the appropriate clothes, toiletries, and personal goods, you will be able to continue your trip without interruption.

Travel Aid: Travel insurance often includes 24-hour travel aid services, giving you access to a specialized hotline in the event of an emergency or a travel-related question. Having travel assistance guarantees that you have expert support at your fingertips, whether you need aid discovering local medical services, managing unexpected situations, or seeking travel guidance.

Extra Coverage Options: Depending on your travel insurance policy, you may be able to purchase extra coverage. These may include coverage for flight delays, missing connections, rental vehicle protection, and other services. It is important to thoroughly evaluate your policy and understand the precise coverage provided to adjust it to your requirements.

As a visitor in Calgary, having travel insurance provides practical safety and peace of mind, enabling you to confidently experience the city. Remember to read your policy thoroughly, understand the terms and conditions, and have your insurance information conveniently available throughout your vacation. With travel insurance, you can concentrate on making amazing memories and experiencing everything that Calgary has to offer.

Tips For Selecting Travel Insurance

Here are some suggestions for selecting travel insurance in Calgary:

Compare plans from various providers: Because there are several travel insurance companies, it is important to compare policies before purchasing one. Make careful you read the tiny print and understand what is and is not covered.

Purchase your insurance coverage as soon as you schedule your trip: This will protect you against any unanticipated circumstances that may arise before your journey.

Check that your insurance covers all of your activities: If you intend on participating in any activities that may need extra coverage, such as skiing or hiking, ensure that your policy covers them.

Keep your insurance information in a secure location: You will need your insurance details on hand if you need to submit a claim.

Travel insurance is an essential aspect of any vacation preparation. You may protect yourself against financial loss in the case of an unforeseen occurrence by taking the time to evaluate plans and choose the best one for you.

Factors To Consider Before Choosing Travel Insurance

There are several travel insurance plans available, therefore it is important to compare them before buying one. When selecting travel insurance coverage, consider the following factors:

The amount of protection you need.
The policy's price.
The terms and conditions of the policy.
The insurance company's reputation.

It's also a good idea to get travel insurance as soon as you arrange your trip. This is because most travel insurance plans do not cover incidents that occur before the purchase of the policy.

Recommended Platforms to Source From

The following are some reliable travel insurance firms that provide plans for visitors visiting Calgary:

- AMA Travel
- Alberta Blue Cross
- Sharp Insurance
- Westland Insurance Company
- Insubuy

Here are some additional suggestions for obtaining travel insurance:

- Before you buy the insurance, thoroughly read it. Check the terms and conditions to ensure you understand what is and is not covered.

- Compare insurance from several providers to discover the best coverage for your need.
- Purchase your coverage at the same time you plan your trip.
- Take a copy of your insurance policy with you on your journey.
- Reach your insurance company carrier if you have any queries.

CHAPTER 11: CONCLUSION

Finally, Calgary has shown to be a city of boundless potential, enthralling tourists with its dynamic combination of urban sophistication and natural beauty. My visit to Calgary as a visitor has been nothing short of fantastic.

Calgary provides a broad selection of experiences that appeal to any traveler's preferences, from the beautiful Rocky Mountains that give a stunning background to the city's skyline to the lively neighborhoods and busy streets.

The city's attractions made an unforgettable impression on my trip. Every moment was filled with wonder and excitement, whether it was exploring the Calgary Zoo and being awestruck by the variety of wildlife, immersing myself in the rich history at the Heritage Park Historical Village, or delving into the world of science and discovery at the Telus Spark Science Centre.

Calgary's festivities and festivals gave a distinctive touch to my vacation. Each event provided a unique view into the city's lively character, from the exhilarating atmosphere of the Calgary Stampede, where I observed exciting rodeo events and celebrated Western culture, to the stunning fireworks displays at GlobalFest.

With its vast mix of tastes, Calgary's food culture enticed my taste buds. The city's eating choices never fail to please, from relishing gourmet cuisine at world-class restaurants to indulging in local specialties at food markets and festivals.

Above all, the kindness and genuine friendliness of the people of Calgary made my visit memorable. From warm talks with neighbors to welcome grins at every turn, Calgary's citizens have made me feel at home in their dynamic town.

As I say goodbye to this amazing city, I take with me fond memories, increased knowledge, and a feeling of appreciation for the incredible experiences Calgary has offered. Calgary has surpassed my expectations and captivated my heart, from its magnificent scenery to its dynamic culture. Until we meet again, in Calgary, I will cherish the memories we had, and the city will have a particular place in my travels.

FQAs

Where Can I Find Additional Information and Travel Assistance?

To guarantee a smooth and pleasurable journey while visiting Calgary, it is important to have access to credible sources of information and travel support. Here are some venues in Calgary where you may get more information and request travel assistance:

Visitor Information Centers: Calgary has numerous visitor information centers that give travelers with a multitude of materials. The main Visitor Information Centre is situated at 414 7th Street SW in downtown Calgary. Brochures, maps, and trained personnel are available here to answer your questions, provide suggestions, and give up-to-date information on attractions, events, and transportation.

Online Resources: Tourism Calgary's official website is a great online resource that gives complete information on attractions, lodging, food, events, and more. The website provides travel guides, itineraries, and practical advice to assist you in planning your vacation to Calgary. Various travel forums and review websites may also provide insights and personal experiences shared by other travelers.

Travel Apps: While touring Calgary, use travel apps to obtain real-time information, maps, and suggestions. Visit Calgary, Google Maps, and TripAdvisor, for example, may give information on area attractions, restaurants, transit alternatives, and user reviews.

Hotel Concierge: If you are staying in a Calgary hotel, the concierge desk might be a useful resource. They can provide you with information about local attractions, transit alternatives, and restaurant suggestions, and help you make bookings or arrange trips. The hotel concierge is trained to help guests and may provide unique recommendations based on your preferences and interests.

Local Transportation Authorities: The official website of Calgary Transit provides detailed information about the city's transportation system, including bus routes, CTrain timetables, and rates. The website contains current information about public transportation services, maps, and trip-planning tools.

Consulates and Embassies: You may contact your country's consulate or embassy in Calgary for help with travel paperwork, emergency circumstances, or other diplomatic services. They may provide advice, assistance, and information particular to your nation of origin.

In the event of an emergency or need for urgent travel assistance, contact local authorities such as the Calgary Police Service (call 911 in an emergency) or your country's embassy/consulate.

You may gain useful information, make educated choices, and guarantee a pleasant and enjoyable stay to

Calgary by using these tools and getting help when necessary.

Here are some resources for extra information and travel aid in Calgary:

Tourist Calgary is the city's official tourist agency. They provide visitors with a number of resources, including

- A comprehensive website offering information on all elements of tourism in Calgary.
- A travel assistance hotline
- In the heart of downtown Calgary, there is a tourist information center.

The city's public transportation system is known as Calgary Transit. They provide a wide range of services, including

Buses

Trains

C-Train is a light rail system.

Transportation that is easily accessible

Visitors may find a range of information on the City of Calgary website, including:

A schedule of attractions and activities

Maps and instructions

Information about visitor safety

The Calgary Stampede is a world-renowned rodeo and event held every July. They provide visitors with a range of information, including

A webpage containing Stampede information.

Stampede Park has a tourist information center.

You may also get more information and travel advice by going to the following websites:

Travel to Calgary

The Calgary Stampede

Calgary Transit

The City of Calgary

If you have any particular queries or need assistance organizing your vacation, please call 1-800-661-1678 or visit their website.

Are there any Safety Tips and Precautions?

When visiting Calgary as a tourist, it is important to prioritize your safety and take the required steps to guarantee a safe and enjoyable vacation. Here are some safety measures and ideas to keep in mind:

Maintain Situational Awareness: Maintain situational awareness at all times. Be aware of your surroundings, particularly in congested locations, public transit, and tourist destinations. Avoid exhibiting valuable items or big sums of money, since this may draw unwelcome attention.

Safe Your possessions: To avoid theft, keep your possessions safe. Carry your valuables in a money belt or a safe bag, and never leave them alone. Be aware of pickpockets in public places and keep your stuff near to you.

Plan Your Itinerary: Before visiting Calgary, make a plan and study the sites you want to visit. Learn about the communities, transit routes, and any safety hazards.

Keep to well-lit and popular locations, particularly at night.

Use Licensed Taxis or Rideshare Services: When utilizing transportation services, consider licensed taxis or renowned ridesharing services such as Uber or Lyft. Verify the driver's identity and that they are using the approved corporate app or car marks. Accepting transportation from unlicensed or unauthorized persons should be avoided.

Be Wary of Public Wi-Fi: Use public Wi-Fi networks with care, particularly when viewing sensitive information or doing online transactions. Use a virtual private network (VPN) to secure your data and personal information, and avoid accessing important accounts on public networks.

Follow Traffic Laws and Cross Streets Safely: Use designated crosswalks and traffic lights while crossing streets. Keep in mind that traffic in Calgary is on the right. Even if the pedestrian signal shows that it is safe to go, look in both directions before crossing.

Drink sensibly: If you must consume alcohol, do it sensibly. Keep your boundaries in mind and prevent binge drinking. Always keep an eye on your drink and be wary about taking beverages from strangers. When out at night, it's usually a good idea to go with a trusted companion.

Emergency Preparedness: Learn the emergency contact numbers in Calgary, including 911 in an emergency. Maintain a copy of your passport, travel insurance information, and critical contact information in a safe place. Keep up to date on local emergency protocols and any relevant safety advice.

Remember that these are basic principles, and it's important to remain up to current on the most recent information from authoritative sources addressing Calgary-specific safety issues and travel warnings. You may have a safe and pleasurable tourist experience in

Calgary by being proactive, alert, and taking the appropriate steps.

How do I Book Tickets For Attractions or Events in Calgary?

Tickets for Calgary attractions or events may be purchased in a variety of ways. Here's a quick rundown on how to book tickets:

Visit the official websites of the attractions or events that you intend to attend. On the website, look for a "Tickets" or "Buy Tickets" area and follow the instructions to choose your preferred day, time, and quantity of tickets. You will get your e-tickets or confirmation after making your payment online.

Ticketmaster, Eventbrite, and StubHub are some examples of online ticketing services. Search for the exact attraction or event you want to attend, choose your tickets, and pay online. Typically, you will get e-tickets or a confirmation email.

On-Site Ticket Booths: Some attractions or events include on-site ticket booths or box offices where you may buy tickets. Simply go to the location, verify availability, and make your purchase in person. Payment is normally done in cash or by credit card.

Local Travel Agents: Contact Calgary's local travel agents or tour operators. They may be able to get reduced tickets or special packages that contain various attractions or activities. Inquire with them about ticket availability and make your reservation.

If you are unable to discover online booking options, contact the venue directly by phone or email. Inquire about ticket availability and any special needs. They will walk you through the booking process and give you with payment and ticket-collecting details.

Before making a purchase, remember to verify the individual attraction or event's booking regulations, such as refund or exchange policies. To ensure your desired day and time, it is suggested that you purchase your tickets in advance, particularly for popular attractions or events.

What is the distance between Calgary and Banff National Park?

Calgary lies around 120 kilometers (75 miles) east of Banff National Park. Depending on traffic and road conditions, the travel time between the two locations is around 1.5 to 2 hours.

How can I get to know the Rocky Mountains from Calgary?

A day trip or multi-day excursion to Banff National Park, Jasper National Park, or Kananaskis Country from Calgary is an easy way to discover the Rocky

Mountains. There are guided excursions, rental vehicles, and self-driving choices for exploring spectacular mountain landscapes, lakes, and animals.

Are there any appropriate attractions for families with children?

Yes, there are various family-friendly attractions in Calgary. Families like visiting the Calgary Zoo, Telus Spark Science Centre, Calaway Park amusement park, and the Aerospace Museum. In addition, there are several parks, playgrounds, and indoor play facilities located around the city.

How can I get an overview of Calgary's arts and cultural scene?

The Arts Commons, which has multiple theaters and performance venues, is a great place to learn about Calgary's arts and cultural sector. The Glenbow Museum and the National Music Centre's Studio Bell are also fantastic locations for art and music fans. You may also visit the city's art galleries, live music events, and local theatrical shows.

Can I drink Calgary's tap water?

Yes, Calgary has safe drinking water from high-quality tap water. In Calgary, you may drink tap water with confidence. Refillable water bottles are popular and promoted for environmental reasons.

What are some of the best day excursions from Calgary?

There are numerous lovely day trip spots close to Calgary. To experience the region's natural and cultural features, consider visiting Drumheller (renowned for its dinosaur fossils and Badlands landscapes), Canmore (a lovely mountain town), or Head-Smashed-In Buffalo Jump (a UNESCO World Heritage Site).

Where can I learn about upcoming public events and festivals in my area?

Various sites provide information on local public events and festivals in Calgary. For the most up-to-date information on future events, check Tourism Calgary's official website, local event calendars, community notice boards, and social media pages of local groups, or visit tourist information centers.

What are the public parking alternatives in Calgary?

Calgary has both street parking and parking facilities across the city. For street parking, parking meters or pay-and-display machines are commonly utilized, while parking garages and lots offer hourly or daily charges. Check parking signs for any additional limitations or requirements.

Is there anything free or low-cost to do in Calgary?

Yes, there are many free or low-cost activities in Calgary. Explore the city's parks, see the public artworks, stroll along the Bow River Pathway, attend free festivals or events, and visit the Calgary Public Library, which has a variety of programs and activities.

What is the best way to go from Calgary International Airport to downtown?

There are many ways to go from Calgary International Airport to downtown. Taking a cab, using ridesharing services like Uber or Lyft, or using the Calgary Transit Airport Shuttle or public bus lines are the most convenient choices.

What are my alternatives for free Wi-Fi in Calgary?

Calgary offers free public Wi-Fi in a variety of areas, including public libraries, parks, and municipal buildings. Customers may use free Wi-Fi at many coffee shops, restaurants, and retail complexes. Furthermore, several mobile service providers give Wi-Fi hotspots to their users in certain places.

Is smoking or cannabis usage restricted or regulated in Calgary?

In Calgary, smoking and cannabis use are governed by legislation established by the City of Calgary and the Alberta Provincial Government. It is critical to adhere to authorized smoking places, respect public spaces, and observe any special smoking or cannabis use restrictions.

What are the current hours and limitations for Calgary's attractions, restaurants, and shops?

Because of the dynamic nature of COVID-19, operation hours and limits for Calgary's attractions, restaurants, and stores may fluctuate. It is best to consult the official websites or directly contact particular businesses to learn about their current working hours, reservation rules, and any limits or guidelines in place.

These are just a handful of the more common inquiries that travelers have while visiting Calgary. During your journey, be sure to use official tourist resources, visitor information centers, and internet platforms to get the most up-to-date and correct information.

Printed in Great Britain
by Amazon

27595654R00089